# Inside the House of David

# Inside the House of David

A Commentary on II Samuel

By

Bill Hawkins

© 2020 by Revolutionary Insights

ISBN: Softcover 978-1-7357405-2-2
ISBN: E-book 978-1-7357405-3-9

All rights reserved by the publisher. No part of this book may be reproduced or transmitted in any form or by any means, electronic or mechanical, including photocopying, recording, or by any information storage and retrieval system, without permission in writing from the copyright owner, except for brief quotations in critical reviews and articles.

Printed in the United States of America

Cover Design: Melissa Altizer

Scripture Quotations of King James Version taken from

https://www.kingjamesbibleonline.org

# Acknowledgments

Over the years several people influenced me in the writing of this book. My parents raised me with Christian principles and were an example before me. Chuck Arney, my youth pastor, led me to salvation by explaining the importance of eternal security. In my young adult years in Ft. Pierce, Florida, W. L. Cooley was a great teaching Pastor who helped me appreciate the depths of the Bible. My former father-in-law, Carl Harris, puzzled me as a young man due to his love of the Bible and his ability to study for hours. Thankfully, I too was able to gain a love for the Word of God once my knees hit the ground and I swallowed my pride and sought God for answers. Afterwards, God sent Sherry into my life and we began studying the Bible together. She and others encouraged me by saying God had given me keen insights on the Bible. She eventually encouraged me to start Revolutionary Insights to share my love for the Bible, politics, and history. Thanks also go out to the countless other people over the years who I ever taught or had discussions with that helped me to hone my thoughts. Finally, I would like to thank Rush Limbaugh for speaking the truth through his radio show during the days when conservative thoughts were not being heard or allowed. His success showed the rest of us that we are not alone.

# Other Books by Bill Hawkins

*Prickett's Fort* – A frontier novel set on the Appalachian frontier of 1778. Based on two true stories. A family friendly novel.

*Where's the Party?* – A book which shows where America's political parties stand in relation to the Ten Commandments.

*Revolutionary Insights Podcast* – Commentary on the three areas of Christianity, Politics and History.

www.revolutionaryinsights.com

# Preface

When one falls in love with the Word of God, it changes the way that person reads the Bible. The reader pauses and looks deeper, searching for nuggets of wisdom buried within its depths that only the patient miner can unearth out of a keen desire to know God.

This commentary on II Samuel is the fruit of one such study. It's not written as a scholarly piece designed to impress the reader with linguistic gymnastics, but rather it's written with a flow easy to read and understand.

This book has no new revelations, but it does have insights that will cause the reader to pause and reflect. One example concerns the root cause of David's sin. Most people blame the lusting of King David for Bathsheba, but in truth the root was something much closer to home.

That is why the book is entitled, *Inside the House of David*. The reader will come to understand the importance of David's houses. In Chapter One we find the house given to him by the Philistines was burned to the ground. David's next house was built for him by the King of Tyre and this is the house that led to David's fall into sin. Then there is the House of David, his posterity, which was fulfilled when Jesus Christ set himself up to be the last king to sit on David's throne. The final house referred to is appropriately the House of God.

The book covers the period from when David became King of Israel until his death forty years later. This forty-year period reveals David, the man, and at the same time, it reveals God. We see David as he is, as we all are, flawed men who sometimes attempt great things through faith.

Some may want to call David a man of contradictions because he was a man who ordered the murder of one of his own loyal soldiers, yet God called him a man after his own heart. How can that be?

David was just like us in that he had flaws. What we hope to learn from David is not how to be a perfect saint, but how to be a man after God's own heart while living an imperfect life.

Is the above a contradiction? No, it is a comforting insight to know that God does not demand perfection from us while we attempt to live the Christian life.


Bill Hawkins

November 20, 2020

Lynchburg, VA

# Table of Contents

Chapter 1 ............................................................................ 1
   The King is Dead, Long Live the King

Chapter 2 ............................................................................ 9
   Civil War

Chapter 3 .......................................................................... 17
   Of Kings and Generals

Chapter 4 .......................................................................... 25
   Assassination of a King

Chapter 5 .......................................................................... 29
   The United Kingdom

Chapter 6 .......................................................................... 37
   The Ark of God

Chapter 7 .......................................................................... 45
   The Davidic Covenant

Chapter 8 .......................................................................... 51
   Peace in the Kingdom

Chapter 9 .......................................................................... 57
   For the Love of Jonathan

Chapter 10 ........................................................................ 63
   The Warrior King

Chapter 11 ........................................................................ 69
   The Edge of Darkness

Chapter 12 ........................................................................ 81
   Repentance

Chapter 13 ........................................................................ 89
    Example to Our Children

Chapter 14 ........................................................................ 99
    To Restore a Son

Chapter 15 ...................................................................... 107
    A Family Divided

Chapter 16 ...................................................................... 115
    Lies and Curses

Chapter 17 ...................................................................... 121
    Confounding the Enemy

Chapter 18 ...................................................................... 129
    Winning a Battle and Losing a Son

Chapter 19 ...................................................................... 137
    Contempt for the King

Chapter 20 ...................................................................... 147
    Yet Another Revolt

Chapter 21 ...................................................................... 155
    Saul's Sin Visits David

Chapter 22 ...................................................................... 161
    Song of Deliverance

Chapter 23 ...................................................................... 169
    Rosebud

Chapter 24 ...................................................................... 177
    Subtraction by Addition

Appendix ........................................................................ 185
    Trial of the Amalekite

# Chapter 1

## The King is Dead, Long Live the King

Years ago, I had some teens in my Bible class say that their teacher at our local public high school insisted there were contradictions in the Bible. Having studied the Bible for years and being unable to find even one contradiction, I marveled that their teacher, who was not a dedicated reader of the Bible, could have made such a claim. So, I asked them about their teacher's claim, and they pointed out this chapter in II Samuel as the proof their teacher gave them of this apparent error in the Bible. Being a firm believer in the inerrancy of the Word of God, and not being familiar with the alleged contradiction at the time, I saw this as an opportunity to teach these teens how to discover truth in real time without studying the alleged contradiction beforehand.

Was I worried I might not be able to prove to these teens there was no contradiction?

Not at all. I trust God when he says he will preserve his Word. *"Heaven and earth shall pass away, but my words shall not pass away"* (Matthew 24:35). So, all I had to do was let them discover which was right - the teacher who claimed there was a contradiction in the Bible or the inerrant Word of God.

# Inside the House of David

## II Samuel Chapter I

*1 Now it came to pass after the death of Saul, when David was returned from the slaughter of the Amalekites, and David had abode two days in Ziklag;*

*2 It came even to pass on the third day, that, behold, a man came out of the camp from Saul with his clothes rent, and earth upon his head: and so it was, when he came to David, that he fell to the earth, and did obeisance.*

*3 And David said unto him, From whence comest thou? And he said unto him, Out of the camp of Israel am I escaped.*

*4 And David said unto him, How went the matter? I pray thee, tell me. And he answered, That the people are fled from the battle, and many of the people also are fallen and dead; and Saul and Jonathan his son are dead also.*

*5 And David said unto the young man that told him, How knowest thou that Saul and Jonathan his son be dead?*

*6 And the young man that told him said, As I happened by chance upon mount Gilboa, behold, Saul leaned upon his spear; and, lo, the chariots and horsemen followed hard after him.*

*7 And when he looked behind him, he saw me, and called unto me. And I answered, Here am I.*

*8 And he said unto me, Who art thou? And I answered him, I am an Amalekite.*

*9 He said unto me again, Stand, I pray thee, upon me, and slay me: for anguish is come upon me, because my life is yet whole in me.*

*10 So I stood upon him, and slew him, because I was sure that he could not live after that he was fallen: and I took the crown that was upon his head, and the bracelet that was on his arm, and have brought them hither unto my lord.*

## The King is Dead, Long Live the King

Chapter One begins with David having returned to Ziklag after having pursued the Amalekites and rescuing all the families they had stolen during the attack on David's village, as revealed in I Samuel Chapter 30. They had only been back two days when a man stumbled into Ziklag, the current home of David, which had been given to him by Achish, a Philistine.

The man appeared to be in mourning, with his clothes rent and ashes on his head. When David asked the man where he was from, he said he had managed to escape the camp of Israel.

I'm sure David's heart must have raced since he would have been eager to hear news of the battle in which the Philistines would not allow him to fight *9 "And Achish answered and said to David, I know that thou art good in my sight, as an angel of God: notwithstanding the princes of the Philistines have said, He shall not go up with us to the battle. 10 Wherefore now rise up early in the morning with thy master's servants that are come with thee: and as soon as ye be up early in the morning, and have light, depart. 11 So David and his men rose up early to depart in the morning, to return into the land of the Philistines. And the Philistines went up to Jezreel"* (I Samuel 29:9-11). When David asked how the battle went, the man informed him that Israel had been routed and that Saul was dead.

This was not the news David had hoped for, so David asked him how he knew Saul was dead, and in verse 10 the Amalekite said he had killed him at Saul's request.

This was the verse that the ignorant teacher told the teens was a contradiction in the Bible. Was this something the teacher had searched out himself and discovered? No, he had read it elsewhere and instead of searching the matter for himself, he put his faith in the writing of a man who didn't want to believe the Bible, instead of the writing of God. His predisposition was to believe the lie because he wanted to believe the lie. The alternative would have been to face God, which would cause him to face himself. His pride wouldn't allow him to admit he needed a savior, so he chose to believe the lie, and sadly, spread it to teens.

So, what is the alleged contradiction? According to this unbelieving teacher, I Samuel 31:4 and I Chronicles 10:4, claim that Saul's armor-bearer killed Saul. *"Then said Saul unto his armourbearer, Draw thy sword, and thrust me through therewith; lest these uncircumcised come and thrust me through, and abuse me. But his armourbearer would not; for he was sore afraid. Therefore Saul took a sword, and fell upon it"* (I Samuel 31:4). *"Then said Saul to his armourbearer, Draw thy sword, and thrust me through therewith; lest these uncircumcised come and abuse me. But his armourbearer would not; for he was sore afraid. So Saul took a sword, and fell upon it"* (I Chronicles 10:4). Of course, if you actually read those two verses, it does not say that at all. The teacher was the one wrong here, in more than one way, when he said the Bible contradicted itself. It wasn't the armor-bearer that killed Saul; in those same verses, we find that Saul fell on his sword.

However, there still appears to be a contradiction. In the two aforementioned verses Saul fell on his sword, but in II Samuel 1:10 the Amalekite claimed he did the deed. So, if Saul fell on his sword, why then did the man here in II Samuel claim he killed Saul at the request of Saul? The man lied; thus, the Bible contains a lie because it records the lie. Incidentally, the first lie the Bible contains is when Satan deceives Eve and tells her if she eats of the fruit, she will not die. So yes, the Bible does contain lies, the lies of others as recorded in the infallible Word of God.

How did David know the man was lying? The man's story simply didn't add up. In verse 6 he claims he just happened to be at Gilboa, where Saul died. Why would a man be on a battlefield unless he was participating in the battle? The man knew this, and so he tried to make it sound like he was on Israel's side in the battle. Remember in verse 3 he had said he had escaped from the camp of Israel as if he was part of the camp. The word "escape" betrayed him to be an enemy of Israel instead of a friend. The idea that an Amalekite was fighting with Israel was another lie because in I Samuel 30:13-14, David was given intelligence by the Egyptian, who had been left to die by the Amalekites, that those very same Amalekites had invaded Judah and were fighting against Saul, not with him. *13 "And David said unto him, To whom belongest thou? and whence art thou? And he said, I am a young man of Egypt, servant to an Amalekite; and my master left me, because three days agone I fell sick. 14 We made an invasion upon the south of the Cherethites, and upon the coast which belongeth to Judah, and upon the south of Caleb; and we burned Ziklag with fire."* The man also admitted he was an Amalekite, the very people that David had just finished slaughtering after they had attacked and burned Ziklag.

Also, the man said that Saul was being pursued and called behind him to ask the man to kill him. If Saul was being pursued and called to the man behind him, then that man must have been one of his pursuers. The man even admitted to taking Saul's crown and the bracelet off his arm. He said he did so because he wanted to find David and give it to him.

David knew better than to believe this man because his own words betrayed him. He was an Amalekite, who was at war with Israel. He was behind Saul as Saul fled, meaning he was pursuing Saul. When he came upon the body, he then stole the crown and bracelet and was on his way back to his people, and to get there, he had to pass through Ziklag, which he apparently thought was going to be empty because he may have heard it had been destroyed.

Note that the Amalekites were a nomadic people that lived in the area of the Negev Desert, including the area east of the Gulf of Aqaba. Ziklag was between Israel and the region where the Amalekites dwelt. So when the man told David he was bringing the crown to him, it was easy to see through the lie. He wasn't going to Ziklag, he was going home. (See Appendix)

*11 Then David took hold on his clothes, and rent them; and likewise all the men that were with him:*

*12 And they mourned, and wept, and fasted until even, for Saul, and for Jonathan his son, and for the people of the LORD, and for the house of Israel; because they were fallen by the sword.*

## Inside the House of David

*13 And David said unto the young man that told him, Whence art thou? And he answered, I am the son of a stranger, an Amalekite.*

*14 And David said unto him, How wast thou not afraid to stretch forth thine hand to destroy the LORD'S anointed?*

*15 And David called one of the young men, and said, Go near, and fall upon him. And he smote him that he died.*

*16 And David said unto him, Thy blood be upon thy head; for thy mouth hath testified against thee, saying, I have slain the LORD'S anointed.*

What was David's reaction upon hearing the news of Saul's death? Keep in mind that Saul had been pursuing David and his men in an effort to kill him. Many people would have taken the occasion to celebrate, but not David. In verses 11 and 12, we see how they mourned and fasted for Saul. Not just for Saul, though. They were also in mourning for the defeat of Israel, and David, in particular, mourned for his close friend, Jonathan.

After the mourning, David returned his attention to the man who had brought the news and asked him again who he was. The man confirmed he was an Amalekite, and then David asked him a more direct (and I'm sure unnerving) question: *"How wast thou not afraid to stretch forth thine hand to destroy the Lord's anointed?"* After all, David would not do it when had the chance, nor would Saul's Armor bearer even after Saul asked him to; yet, this Amalekite claimed to have killed Saul. *"And he said unto his men, The LORD forbid that I should do this thing unto my master, the LORD'S anointed, to stretch forth mine hand against him, seeing he is the anointed of the LORD"* (I Samuel 24:6).

Why would he make the claim when he didn't do it, since Saul fell on his own sword? How else could he explain how he had come into possession of the crown and bracelet of Saul? David knew the man had been lying about nearly everything he said, so in verse 15, David ordered one of his young men to execute the Amalekite for his actions against not only Saul but against the nation of Israel. In verse 16, David lets it be known that the man's own words condemned him.

*17 And David lamented with this lamentation over Saul and over Jonathan his son:*

*18 (Also he bade them teach the children of Judah the use of the bow: behold, it is written in the book of Jasher.)*

*19 The beauty of Israel is slain upon thy high places: how are the mighty fallen!*

*20 Tell it not in Gath, publish it not in the streets of Askelon; lest the daughters of the Philistines rejoice, lest the daughters of the uncircumcised triumph.*

*21 Ye mountains of Gilboa, let there be no dew, neither let there be rain, upon you, nor fields of offerings: for there the shield of the mighty is vilely cast away, the shield of Saul, as though he had not been anointed with oil.*

*22 From the blood of the slain, from the fat of the mighty, the bow of Jonathan turned not back, and the sword of Saul returned not empty.*

*23 Saul and Jonathan were lovely and pleasant in their lives, and in their death they were not divided: they were swifter than eagles, they were stronger than lions.*

*24 Ye daughters of Israel, weep over Saul, who clothed you in scarlet, with other delights, who put on ornaments of gold upon your apparel.*

*25 How are the mighty fallen in the midst of the battle! O Jonathan, thou wast slain in thine high places.*

*26 I am distressed for thee, my brother Jonathan: very pleasant hast thou been unto me: thy love to me was wonderful, passing the love of women.*

*27 How are the mighty fallen, and the weapons of war perished!*

## Inside the House of David

Verses 17-27 are a heartfelt eulogy for Saul, but especially so for Jonathan, David's dear friend. The first thing we notice in verse 18, however, is how from this tragedy, David learns a valuable lesson and determines Israel will benefit from it. He will teach his men how to use the bow. Jonathan had mastered the weapon, and Saul was an expert with the sword; however, in war, it takes more than what a few can master. I'm sure this vow worked very well for David as he expanded his kingdom and made this time the beginning of the period known as the Golden Age of Israel.

Verse 26 is especially touching as David expresses his love for Jonathan, which surpassed that of even women. In today's world, some might want to suggest a homosexual relationship between the two men in an effort to justify their acceptance of the sin God calls an abomination. However, this was not the case.

In 2015 my father told me about his experience in the Korean War, which he had never shared with me before. My father fought two years in Korea during the height of the conflict. He said he wanted to go back because he had bonded with those men with whom he had shared both life and death. He said that when he came back home and returned to his family in the same house where he had been born and raised along with ten other children, he felt like a stranger, for his real family had been the men he had fought side by side with on the Korean Peninsula.

David had that kind of bond with Jonathan, a closeness that is greater than that of a woman. Jonathan was a mighty man to David, and so David pens the line through the inspiration of God, *"How the mighty are fallen..."*

# Chapter 2

## Civil War

*II Samuel Chapter II*

*1 And it came to pass after this, that David enquired of the LORD, saying, Shall I go up into any of the cities of Judah? And the LORD said unto him, Go up. And David said, Whither shall I go up? And he said, Unto Hebron.*

*2 So David went up thither, and his two wives also, Ahinoam the Jezreelitess, and Abigail Nabal's wife the Carmelite.*

*3 And his men that were with him did David bring up, every man with his household: and they dwelt in the cities of Hebron.*

*4 And the men of Judah came, and there they anointed David king over the house of Judah. And they told David, saying, That the men of Jabeshgilead were they that buried Saul.*

*5 And David sent messengers unto the men of Jabeshgilead, and said unto them, Blessed be ye of the LORD, that ye have shewed this kindness unto your lord, even unto Saul, and have buried him.*

*6 And now the LORD shew kindness and truth unto you: and I also will requite you this kindness, because ye have done this thing.*

*7 Therefore now let your hands be strengthened, and be ye valiant: for your master Saul is dead, and also the house of Judah have anointed me king over them.*

*8 But Abner the son of Ner, captain of Saul's host, took Ishbosheth the son of Saul, and brought him over to Mahanaim;*

*9 And made him king over Gilead, and over the Ashurites, and over Jezreel, and over Ephraim, and over Benjamin, and over all Israel.*

*10 Ishbosheth Saul's son was forty years old when he began to reign over Israel, and reigned two years. But the house of Judah followed David.*

*11 And the time that David was king in Hebron over the house of Judah was seven years and six months.*

Chapter two begins with David asking God if he should go up to Judah, but when the answer was yes, he did not quickly rush off, instead he asked to which city God wanted him to go. David as a great king and we think of great kings as being able to easily make decisions. Saul, whom David replaced as king, had a very real problem with making decisions; whereas David allowed God to make his decisions. The one major decision David made, which we all would be wiser to do the same, was he asked God for answers. Not only did he ask God if he should go, he went a step further and asked where he should go.

### A Man After God's Own Heart

**David went to God for answers to his questions and he asked God to even decide the details. He let God make the decisions.**

It doesn't make a person weaker if he seeks God's will for his life and allows God to make decisions. It shows faith and strength of character to not be afraid to admit you don't not know everything and that God does. David didn't know the future and God did, so it made a great deal more sense to allow God to lead, rather than attempt something for which he couldn't know the outcome. God does know the outcome, so trust Him with it.

God sends David, his family and his men to dwell in Hebron. It won't be long until the leaders of Judah come and anoint David King of Judah. Judah was often mentioned apart from the rest of Israel. No other tribe was mentioned in this same way where different tribes had different kings. Saul was of the tribe of Benjamin, but he was king over all of Israel. David was of the tribe of Judah, so it's natural that they would accept him as king, but it wasn't to be the same for the other tribes of Israel. This was a pretext of what was to become between the divided kingdoms of Judah and Israel.

As a matter of a fact, Israel chose someone else to reign over them who was not chosen of God as David had been when Samuel anointed him to be King of Israel in I Samuel Chapter 16 where it says in verses 12 and 13, *"And he sent, and brought him in. Now he was ruddy, and withal of a beautiful countenance, and goodly to look to. And the LORD said, Arise, anoint him: for this is he. Then Samuel took the horn of oil, and anointed him in the midst of his brethren: and the Spirit of the LORD came upon David from that day forward. So Samuel rose up, and went to Ramah."*

Saul, who had been king when Samuel anointed David, was now dead. One would think that Israel would go ahead and pick David to be their next king, but instead Abner, who had served as Saul's Captain of the Host, brought Ishbosheth, the son of Saul, and set him up as king over Israel. He would have been king over Judah too, except that Judah had already set David up to be their king.

This begs the question, why didn't Israel choose God's anointed - David? After all, it seems Israel is defying the wishes of God by not accepting David as their king. Go back and read all of I Samuel chapter 16 and find where the anointing of David to be the next king is announced to all of Israel. The only people who knew Samuel had anointed David were the leaders of Bethlehem and David's father and brothers.

This event was not announced because Samuel was afraid to anger Saul because he was afraid Saul would have him killed. As far as the nation of Israel was concerned, the next King of Israel needed to come from the hereditary line of Saul. Therefore, to them, it was only natural that Ishbosheth would become the next King of Israel, as had been his father, Saul.

God does not have to reveal His plans to people and then hope they listen and implement them. If God wishes something to happen, he does not need the help of man to see it come to fruition.

## Inside the House of David

Verses 5-7 reveals something about, not only David, but about the rest of us as well. David sent messengers to Jabesh-gilead, commending them for rescuing the bodies of Saul and Jonathan and then burying them. He told them he would treat them right for their good deed. However, where in these verses does he actually do anything to bless Jabesh-gilead in a tangible way?

Later in II Samuel we will see how David's conscience is going to be pricked because he should have done more to properly take care of the bodies of Saul and Jonathan. In other words, David made the same mistake many of us do in our Christian walk. How often do we hear of someone in need and then tell them we will pray for them and ask God to bless them, but then fail to assist them in a tangible way? In chapter 21:12-14, we see David do what he should have done here in chapter two, but we will discuss that in more detail once we get to chapter 21.

*12 And Abner the son of Ner, and the servants of Ishbosheth the son of Saul, went out from Mahanaim to Gibeon.*

*13 And Joab the son of Zeruiah, and the servants of David, went out, and met together by the pool of Gibeon: and they sat down, the one on the one side of the pool, and the other on the other side of the pool.*

*14 And Abner said to Joab, Let the young men now arise, and play before us. And Joab said, Let them arise.*

*15 Then there arose and went over by number twelve of Benjamin, which pertained to Ishbosheth the son of Saul, and twelve of the servants of David.*

*16 And they caught every one his fellow by the head, and thrust his sword in his fellow's side; so they fell down together: wherefore that place was called Helkathhazzurim, which is in Gibeon.*

*17 And there was a very sore battle that day; and Abner was beaten, and the men of Israel, before the servants of David.*

*18 And there were three sons of Zeruiah there, Joab, and Abishai, and Asahel: and Asahel was as light of foot as a wild roe.*

*19 And Asahel pursued after Abner; and in going he turned not to the right hand nor to the left from following Abner.*

*20 Then Abner looked behind him, and said, Art thou Asahel? And he answered, I am.*

*21 And Abner said to him, Turn thee aside to thy right hand or to thy left, and lay thee hold on one of the young men, and take thee his armour. But Asahel would not turn aside from following of him.*

*22 And Abner said again to Asahel, Turn thee aside from following me: wherefore should I smite thee to the ground? how then should I hold up my face to Joab thy brother?*

*23 Howbeit he refused to turn aside: wherefore Abner with the hinder end of the spear smote him under the fifth rib, that the spear came out behind him; and he fell down there, and died in the same place: and it came to pass, that as many as came to the place where Asahel fell down and died stood still.*

*24 Joab also and Abishai pursued after Abner: and the sun went down when they were come to the hill of Ammah, that lieth before Giah by the way of the wilderness of Gibeon.*

*25 And the children of Benjamin gathered themselves together after Abner, and became one troop, and stood on the top of an hill.*

*26 Then Abner called to Joab, and said, Shall the sword devour for ever? knowest thou not that it will be bitterness in the latter end? how long shall it be then, ere thou bid the people return from following their brethren?*

*27 And Joab said, As God liveth, unless thou hadst spoken, surely then in the morning the people had gone up every one from following his brother.*

*28 So Joab blew a trumpet, and all the people stood still, and pursued after Israel no more, neither fought they any more.*

*29 And Abner and his men walked all that night through the plain, and passed over Jordan, and went through all Bithron, and they came to Mahanaim.*

*30 And Joab returned from following Abner: and when he had gathered all the people together, there lacked of David's servants nineteen men and Asahel.*

*31 But the servants of David had smitten of Benjamin, and of Abner's men, so that three hundred and threescore men died.*

*32 And they took up Asahel, and buried him in the sepulchre of his father, which was in Bethlehem. And Joab and his men went all night, and they came to Hebron at break of day.*

Since God's people were now ruled by two rulers, David in Judah and Ishbosheth in Israel. Conflict was bound to arise. The tension became thick when the leaders of the two armies met on either side of the pool of Gibeon. I imagine both sides were seeing who would blink first. Finally, Abner suggested letting the young men play together. Of course, by saying play no one expected they were going to break out in a sport. Instead, as soldiers, they were going to try and kill the other.

From Benjamin, the tribe of Ishbosheth, came 12 men. From Judah, the tribe of David, came 12 men. All the young men grabbed the other by the head and thrust their swords into each other, killing all 24. I don't think anyone saw that coming. Worse still, it settled nothing. As a result, the fight extended between both armies.

Ishbosheth's army, led by Abner, was defeated by David's army, led by Joab. After the defeat, Asahel, the younger brother of Joab who was an excellent runner pursues after Abner. He is relentless and ignores Abner when Abner asks him to peel off and pursue another. He didn't ask this of Asahel because he feared him, but because he didn't want to hurt him and as a result, cause Joab anguish.

Asahel, as youth often do, mistook Abner's plea for weakness instead of strength. He would not listen and so Abner stopped suddenly and allowed Asahel to rush upon him and using Asahel's momentum against him, he drove his spear through Asahel, killing him. Joab and his other brother Abishai continued pursuing after Abner until evening when soldiers gathered around Abner on the top of a hill.

Abner was tired, and he did what tired people often do – he gave up. He asked Joab why they had to keep fighting when they are really brothers. Actually, Abner and Joab were cousins, so when Abner asked how long the people would follow their brothers, it meant more than just kin by nation, but actual kin by birth.

In response, Joab ordered the army to stop. Which allowed Abner to make his escape. When they had time to count their losses, Joab had lost 20 men, whereas, Abner had lost 360. That surely sounds like a decisive victory for Judah. However, Joab wasn't celebrating his victory, instead he was burying his younger brother and it was a loss he would not forget. As we shall soon see.

# Chapter 3

## *Of Kings and Generals*

*II Samuel Chapter III*

*1 Now there was long war between the house of Saul and the house of David: but David waxed stronger and stronger, and the house of Saul waxed weaker and weaker.*

*2 And unto David were sons born in Hebron: and his first-born was Amnon, of Ahinoam the Jezreelitess;*

*3 And his second, Chileab, of Abigail the wife of Nabal the Carmelite; and the third, Absalom the son of Maacah the daughter of Talmai king of Geshur;*

*4 And the fourth, Adonijah the son of Haggith; and the fifth, Shephatiah the son of Abital;*

*5 And the sixth, Ithream, by Eglah David's wife. These were born to David in Hebron.*

While the civil war continued to rage between Israel, led by Saul's son, and Judah, led by David, life goes on and David's family begins to grow. His capital is in Hebron and he has six sons born in that city of different mothers. Of those six sons, we will hear much more about the third son, Absalom, who had been birthed by Maacah, the daughter of the King of Geshur, Talmai. We will also see that Maacah appears to have been the kind of mother who engrained a great deal of ambition into her sons. An ambition that clearly showed she cared much more for her sons than her husband.

The husband wife relationship between David and his wives was not the kind of marriage relationship as we think today. According to the Bible, David had many wives, but it only mentions eight of them. He did not have one at a time; he had many at a time. In these Biblical times, having multiple wives was more about political advantage, or a welfare system, than it was love. The marriage with Maacah was one of political advantage. In most other cases, marriage was more about the support of women who, as is still true today, outnumbered the men. Therefore, since women could not support themselves they had to rely on a man for support. As king, David would have the wealth needed to support many women, who became his wives or concubines in return.

*6 And it came to pass, while there was war between the house of Saul and the house of David, that Abner made himself strong for the house of Saul.*

*7 And Saul had a concubine, whose name was Rizpah, the daughter of Aiah: and Ishbosheth said to Abner, Wherefore hast thou gone in unto my father's concubine?*

*8 Then was Abner very wroth for the words of Ishbosheth, and said, Am I a dog's head, which against Judah do shew kindness this day unto the house of Saul thy father, to his brethren, and to his friends, and have not delivered thee into the hand of David, that thou chargest me to day with a fault concerning this woman?*

*9 So do God to Abner, and more also, except, as the LORD hath sworn to David, even so I do to him;*

*10 To translate the kingdom from the house of Saul, and to set up the throne of David over Israel and over Judah, from Dan even to Beersheba.*

*11 And he could not answer Abner a word again, because he feared him.*

As the war goes on, Abner grows in power. So much so that Abner was the real power behind the throne of Israel, and he knew it. So when Ishbosheth comes to him and confronts him about having relations with one of his father's (Saul's) concubines, it angers Abner who in no uncertain terms makes it clear that he has the ability to deliver Ishbosheth's kingdom into the hands of David if he so wishes.

How did Ishbosheth, the King of Israel, react? Did he have Abner arrested and removed from his position, or did he cower in the face of his general? He cowered, and the one thing a man of valor, as was Abner, could not stand was a coward. Therefore, Abner contacted David and offered him the kingdom of Ishbosheth. He knew David was no coward.

*12 And Abner sent messengers to David on his behalf, saying, Whose is the land? saying also, Make thy league with me, and, behold, my hand shall be with thee, to bring about all Israel unto thee.*

*13 And he said, Well; I will make a league with thee: but one thing I require of thee, that is, Thou shalt not see my face, except thou first bring Michal Saul's daughter, when thou comest to see my face.*

*14 And David sent messengers to Ishbosheth Saul's son, saying, Deliver me my wife Michal, which I espoused to me for an hundred foreskins of the Philistines.*

*15 And Ishbosheth sent, and took her from her husband, even from Phaltiel the son of Laish.*

*16 And her husband went with her along weeping behind her to Bahurim. Then said Abner unto him, Go, return. And he returned.*

*17 And Abner had communication with the elders of Israel, saying, Ye sought for David in times past to be king over you:*

*18 Now then do it: for the LORD hath spoken of David, saying, By the hand of my servant David I will save my people Israel out of the hand of the Philistines, and out of the hand of all their enemies.*

*19 And Abner also spake in the ears of Benjamin: and Abner went also to speak in the ears of David in Hebron all that seemed good to Israel, and that seemed good to the whole house of Benjamin.*

*20 So Abner came to David to Hebron, and twenty men with him. And David made Abner and the men that were with him a feast.*

*21 And Abner said unto David, I will arise and go, and will gather all Israel unto my lord the king, that they may make a league with thee, and that thou mayest reign over all that thine heart desireth. And David sent Abner away; and he went in peace.*

*22 And, behold, the servants of David and Joab came from pursuing a troop, and brought in a great spoil with them: but Abner was not with David in Hebron; for he had sent him away, and he was gone in peace.*

*23 When Joab and all the host that was with him were come, they told Joab, saying, Abner the son of Ner came to the king, and he hath sent him away, and he is gone in peace.*

*24 Then Joab came to the king, and said, What hast thou done? behold, Abner came unto thee; why is it that thou hast sent him away, and he is quite gone?*

*25 Thou knowest Abner the son of Ner, that he came to deceive thee, and to know thy going out and thy coming in, and to know all that thou doest.*

*26 And when Joab was come out from David, he sent messengers after Abner, which brought him again from the well of Sirah: but David knew it not.*

*27 And when Abner was returned to Hebron, Joab took him aside in the gate to speak with him quietly, and smote him there under the fifth rib, that he died, for the blood of Asahel his brother.*

David agreed to meet with Abner, but he had one condition. He wanted to see Michal, his very first wife that had been taken away from him by her father Saul. He may have had many wives, but Michal was the first and they had married when David wasn't wealthy. They say we never forget our first love, and David still loved Michal and wanted to see her.

Interestingly, David then sends a message to Ishbosheth telling him to send Michal to him and showing that he had legal grounds for wanting his first wife returned. Why does David do this when he knows that Abner will be bringing her to him? It was a way of proving to everyone, including Abner, that David was stronger than Ishbosheth. In other words, David did not need Abner's help to subjugate Ishbosheth and Israel. This way Abner wouldn't think he was indispensable and that David needed him. Abner would not be the power behind David's throne.

I wonder what the expression was on Abner's face when Ishbosheth tells him to go get Michal and take her to David? He had been out maneuvered, and in a way, put in his place.

When Abner does get Michal to take to David, her husband follows her weeping. He was the man that Saul had given her to when he took her from David during the time David was fleeing for his life. Abner tolerates this for a while, but as soon as he tells the man to go home, the man does as he is told.

Abner has already made the necessary arrangement to turn over Israel to David. He had met with the leaders of all the tribes of Israel, including Benjamin, the tribe of Saul, and they all agreed to let David be their king. Part of the argument used by Abner was that God had said David would deliver them from the Philistines and since they had been willing to follow him in the past, it was now time to do so again. Since they all agreed, Abner now had the power to change his allegiance from Ishbosheth to David, as the rest of Israel was willing to do. Of course, they were only willing to do this when they realized that continuing to fight Judah was futile.

So David prepares a feast for Abner and the 20 men with him. Abner agrees to deliver Israel to David and asks to be allowed to return to Israel to finalize the act. David allows him to go in peace, meaning with his protection.

However, once Joab returns to Hebron and finds out that Abner had been there and that David had allowed him to return to Israel in peace, he was none too pleased with his king and questions and berates him for allowing himself to be deceived, as Joab believed Abner had done.

Joab wasn't one to stand around when he thought someone else may challenge his authority. Abner was his enemy, and he wasn't going to allow him to come in and take his place. So, Joab is going to take matters into his own hands and defy his king. He sends messengers to ask Abner to return to Hebron. Abner does so; probably thinking David wants to speak with him again. However, King David knew nothing of the actions of Joab.

Abner returns and Joab takes him aside and kills him. Not only had Abner been his military adversary, but Joab was avenging his brother who had been killed by Abner in the battle at Gibeon.

*28 And afterward when David heard it, he said, I and my kingdom are guiltless before the LORD for ever from the blood of Abner the son of Ner:*

*29 Let it rest on the head of Joab, and on all his father's house; and let there not fail from the house of Joab one that hath an issue, or that is a leper, or that leaneth on a staff, or that falleth on the sword, or that lacketh bread.*

*30 So Joab and Abishai his brother slew Abner, because he had slain their brother Asahel at Gibeon in the battle.*

*31 And David said to Joab, and to all the people that were with him, Rend your clothes, and gird you with sackcloth, and mourn before Abner. And king David himself followed the bier.*

*32 And they buried Abner in Hebron: and the king lifted up his voice, and wept at the grave of Abner; and all the people wept.*

*33 And the king lamented over Abner, and said, Died Abner as a fool dieth?*

*34 Thy hands were not bound, nor thy feet put into fetters: as a man falleth before wicked men, so fellest thou. And all the people wept again over him.*

*35 And when all the people came to cause David to eat meat while it was yet day, David sware, saying, So do God to me, and more also, if I taste bread, or ought else, till the sun be down.*

*36 And all the people took notice of it, and it pleased them: as whatsoever the king did pleased all the people.*

*37 For all the people and all Israel understood that day that it was not of the king to slay Abner the son of Ner.*

*38 And the king said unto his servants, Know ye not that there is a prince and a great man fallen this day in Israel?*

*39 And I am this day weak, though anointed king; and these men the sons of Zeruiah be too hard for me: the LORD shall reward the doer of evil according to his wickedness.*

Joab was not serving God and he was not serving David, he was serving himself. David was greatly angered by what Joab had done, but he doesn't deal directly with Joab, instead he curses his family and lets it be known that the blood of Abner is on Joab, and not on himself.

David mourns for Abner, and makes Joab also mourn. I'm sure this must have gulled Joab, but he knew better than to anger David any further. It may also appear that Joab got away with his crime, but we will see later that he does pay for what he did. As Christians, we sometimes want immediate gratification by seeing someone who has done wrong suffer immediately for their transgression. However, very few times in scripture do we see God immediately punish an evil doer. More often, God repays evil later, when the wrongdoer most likely thinks God has forgotten and he has gotten away with his wrong. God may delay His judgment, but God is just, and be sure your sins will find you out.

Notice a difference between Joab and David. Joab took matters into his own hands and avenged his brother's death. David knew that vengeance belonged to the Lord, and he was going to allow God to bring judgment on Joab and his brother Abishai.

Sometimes people in church do us wrong and we want to avenge ourselves. It is the natural thing to do. However, we are not to be following the natural man, we are to follow the spiritual man and the spiritual man knows we are to deliver our slights to God and allow him to take care of our problems.

Years ago, I had an older couple in our church who had taken me and my family under their wings. They were friends that my wife and I were going to make god parents over our children. One day they betrayed me and tried to ruin me. I was caught completely off guard and I was obviously incredibly angry at their actions. I remember calling our pastor, whom they had made their accusations to, and asked him what I should do. He counseled me to do as the Bible says and go to my accuser with a witness. I did so and I thought all was well again, but later that night the leader of the family, and a man whom I thought was my friend, again accused me of wrongdoing. I was furious and I again called my pastor and asked him what I should do now, since I had already tried the first method as prescribed by God in the Bible. My pastor asked me what I wanted to do, and I said, "I want God to take vengeance on them." Of course, I thought I was wrong for thinking such thoughts and expected to be admonished by my pastor, but instead he told me to go ahead and pray that way. I was surprised and asked, "But isn't that wrong?" My pastor laughed and said, if that's how you feel, that's how you pray, because you're not going to fool God. He told me to let God take care of the matter and if I was wrong to pray that way, God would let me know in a gentle way. So, I prayed that way. I remember months later asking God to let up on that family who, incidentally, had also turned on the pastor of our church and attempted to split it. God had taken care of the problem in a way I never could have done, and his actions were just and fair to all involved.

Next time you're tempted to seek your own revenge, step aside and ask God to do it. You're not going to fool Him anyway so simply be honest with Him. He knows what's in your heart, so trust Him.

# Chapter 4

## Assassination of a King

*II Samuel, Chapter IV*

*1 And when Saul's son heard that Abner was dead in Hebron, his hands were feeble, and all the Israelites were troubled.*

*2 And Saul's son had two men that were captains of bands: the name of the one was Baanah, and the name of the other Rechab, the sons of Rimmon a Beerothite, of the children of Benjamin: (for Beeroth also was reckoned to Benjamin:*

*3 And the Beerothites fled to Gittaim, and were sojourners there until this day.)*

*4 And Jonathan, Saul's son, had a son that was lame of his feet. He was five years old when the tidings came of Saul and Jonathan out of Jezreel, and his nurse took him up, and fled: and it came to pass, as she made haste to flee, that he fell, and became lame. And his name was Mephibosheth.*

*5 And the sons of Rimmon the Beerothite, Rechab and Baanah, went, and came about the heat of the day to the house of Ishbosheth, who lay on a bed at noon.*

*6 And they came thither into the midst of the house, as though they would have fetched wheat; and they smote him under the fifth rib: and Rechab and Baanah his brother escaped.*

*7 For when they came into the house, he lay on his bed in his bedchamber, and they smote him, and slew him, and beheaded him, and took his head, and gat them away through the plain all night.*

*8 And they brought the head of Ishbosheth unto David to Hebron, and said to the king, Behold the head of Ishbosheth the son of Saul thine enemy, which sought thy life; and the LORD hath avenged my lord the king this day of Saul, and of his seed.*

*9 And David answered Rechab and Baanah his brother, the sons of Rimmon the Beerothite, and said unto them, As the LORD liveth, who hath redeemed my soul out of all adversity,*

*10 When one told me, saying, Behold, Saul is dead, thinking to have brought good tidings, I took hold of him, and slew him in Ziklag, who thought that I would have given him a reward for his tidings:*

*11 How much more, when wicked men have slain a righteous person in his own house upon his bed? shall I not therefore now require his blood of your hand, and take you away from the earth?*

*12 And David commanded his young men, and they slew them, and cut off their hands and their feet, and hanged them up over the pool in Hebron. But they took the head of Ishbosheth, and buried it in the sepulchre of Abner in Hebron.*

The strength behind the throne of Israel was Abner, so when Ishbosheth learned Abner was dead, verse 1 says his hands were feeble and all the Israelites were troubled. If we put our trust in a man, when that man is gone, then fear will grip us. Many of the people of Judah, and later Israel, put their trust in David, but note that the strength behind the throne of Judah was God. However, as Christians, we should never put our trust in a man, even a man of David's caliber. As long as David trusted God and went to Him for his answers, all was well.

### A Man After God's Own Heart

**It was God who was the power behind David's throne because David went to God for his answers and for his power.**

## Assassination of a King

In their fear, two men, captains over troops in the Israeli army, decided they need to take matters into their own hands in the place of Abner and put Israel under the protection of King David in Judah. Fear is an emotion, and anytime we make a decision based on our emotions, those decisions are always wrong. Even if things seem to work out, it was a wrong decision because it may fool us into thinking it is okay to make decisions based on emotions in the future.

Israel had already been willing to make David their king, but these two captains weren't sure of the future, so they decided to help ensure that David would be their next king. If Joab hadn't taken matters into his own hands, then Israel would have already been under the rule of David. And now these two captains take matters into their own hands and it's going to cost them their lives.

The two captains sneak into King Ishbosheth's house and decapitate him so they can prove to David they had done his work for him. They probably thought David would give them a reward for their handiwork. Instead David tells them, just like the Amalekite who brought him the crown and bracelet of Saul, he would require their life for their sin in harming God's anointed.

Was Ishbosheth annointed by God the same way David was when Samuel called him from the House of Jesse? No, he wasn't. Ishbosheth became King because of Abner and because he was the son of Saul. Yet, David still considers him God's annointed. Our leaders are God's annointed and as it says in Hebrews 13:7 *"Obey them that have the rule over you, and submit yourselves: for they watch for your souls, as they that must give account, that they may do it with joy, and not with grief: for that is unprofitable for you."*

Does this include a President of the United States? Yes. Unlike Israel at the time, we have the ability to choose our leaders. We should take advantage of this opportunity provided to us by God to make sure our leaders rule based on Biblical values. If they do not, we are to obey them still, until that leadership conflicts with those values God gave us in the Bible. Then, we are to use our right to vote to choose a different leader. We are also not required to obey the law of men when it conflicts with the law of God.

I once had an immigrant to America ask me if it was wrong to be patriotic. I was astonished by the question, because I couldn't fathom why someone would think it was wrong to love your country. His explanation was that the Germans of the National Socialist German Worker's Party (NAZI's) were patriotic Germans who committed horrible acts against innocent humans in the name of patriotism.

I paused and thought for a minute, because the question was so unexpected, and I had never encountered any question like it before. As I thought about it, I came to realize how important it was to have Godly values being practiced by the citizens of a nation. If our government were to order us to commit acts of murder, as in what the Nazi's did to the Jews in the Holocaust, Godly citizens would refuse to carry out that order. Whereas, citizens that denied God and Biblical values, might obey those orders because to them the highest authority in our lives is government.

As long as our leaders have a fear of God, we need not fear our government. However, once the fear of God has been lost in our country, then it is time to fear our government.

The act of the two captains was cowardly and they had killed a righteous man. Therefore, David had them slain and their hands and feet cut off. Why cut off their hands and feet? Their hands had killed Ishbosheth and then cut off his head. Their feet brought their evil tidings and proof of their evil deed across the plain and to David. So David made them a public example. He also buried the head of Ishbosheth in the sepulcher of Abner. To speculate as to why this was done leads to a myriad of possible explanations.

Verse 4 seems to be misplaced, but we know the Bible is the inspired Word of God, so it must be here for a reason. The reason would appear to be to show that there were no more heirs to the throne from Saul's house. Mephibosheth was crippled, and he had been given refuge in David's house for Jonathan's sake. With the death of Ishbosheth, Saul's line is gone and now David can become the undisputed King of Israel.

# Chapter 5

## *The United Kingdom*

*II Samuel Chapter V*

*1 Then came all the tribes of Israel to David unto Hebron, and spake, saying, Behold, we are thy bone and thy flesh.*

*2 Also in time past, when Saul was king over us, thou wast he that leddest out and broughtest in Israel: and the LORD said to thee, Thou shalt feed my people Israel, and thou shalt be a captain over Israel.*

*3 So all the elders of Israel came to the king to Hebron; and king David made a league with them in Hebron before the LORD: and they anointed David king over Israel.*

*4 David was thirty years old when he began to reign, and he reigned forty years.*

*5 In Hebron he reigned over Judah seven years and six months: and in Jerusalem he reigned thirty and three years over all Israel and Judah.*

Now that Abner is dead, having been killed by Joab, and Ishbosheth is dead, having been killed by two of his captains; the heads of the tribes of Israel come to David and ask him to be their king. They finally admit that God had intended David to be king from the beginning and it was David who led Israel in battle when Saul was king. You would think that since they knew this of David, that they would already have crowned him king. However, we know that God is the creator of the universe and knows the future and cares for us and loves us, but we still, too often, don't trust Him with our life. So ask yourself this question, and be honest, if you were in Israel at the time would you have wanted David to be your king?

To be frank, the answer to that question has already been answered in your life by the answer to this question; do you sincerely trust God with your life? In other words, do you ask him to guide your life and then follow where he leads, or do you walk where you want to go and hope God is okay with the direction you're going?

Now that you've answered that question, and I hope you answered it honestly; otherwise, you're only fooling yourself. We will return to David becoming King over a united Israel. David was thirty years old when he became king over Judah and thirty-seven and a half when he became king over Israel, reigning a total of forty years.

*6 And the king and his men went to Jerusalem unto the Jebusites, the inhabitants of the land: which spake unto David, saying, Except thou take away the blind and the lame, thou shalt not come in hither: thinking, David cannot come in hither.*

*7 Nevertheless David took the strong hold of Zion: the same is the city of David.*

*8 And David said on that day, Whosoever getteth up to the gutter, and smiteth the Jebusites, and the lame and the blind, that are hated of David's soul, he shall be chief and captain. Wherefore they said, The blind and the lame shall not come into the house.*

*9 So David dwelt in the fort, and called it the city of David. And David built round about from Millo and inward.*

David's capital was in the city of Hebron (When Caleb said he wanted that mountain, the mountain was Hebron), but God had another city picked out to be the capital of all Israel and so David moved to take Jerusalem from the Jebusites. When Israel entered the Promised Land, it was divided between the tribes and Jerusalem was within the borders of Benjamin. However, it was close enough to Judah for them to take the city (Judges 1:8), which they did, but the tribe of Benjamin allowed the Jebusites to remain in the city

(Judges 1:21) after Judah withdrew, and over time, the Jebusites regained control. It was a fortified city and not easy to retake, so from the time Israel entered the land until David, it continued to be a Jebusite city, except for the short time that Judah had first taken it upon entering the Promised Land.

The next part of these verses about the blind and the lame is a bit puzzling at first. It says in verse 8 that the blind and lame were hated by David's soul. How could David not have compassion on the blind and the lame? Obviously, this must not have been helpless blind and lame people. So then what is the explanation?

## A Man After God's Own Heart

**Since David was a man after God's own heart, then whatever God hated it is reasonable to think David hated also.**

What is it in the Bible that is blind and lame that God hates? The answer is found in a Psalm God inspired David to write. Psalm 115:5-7 tells us their gods have eyes but see not and have feet but walk not. In other words, the Jebusites were mocking David and his God saying David could not get past their gods that protect their city. Their arrogant faith in their gods led to their downfall. People sometimes show great faith in what they believe, but faith in a lie is foolishness.

Perhaps this arrogant attitude was supposed to make David fear, but he knew their gods were no match for his God, so their attitude meant nothing to him. He tells his men that whosoever overcomes the Jebusites and destroys the lame and blind gods of the Jebusites, then those men will become captains in his army.

The Jebusites had put their misplaced faith in their gods and in their fortified stronghold. David, who did indeed hate their gods, destroyed them and captured the city. He then made what had been the Jebusite stronghold his stronghold and began building the City of David around it. As he grew stronger, those around began to take notice of this young king and his accomplishments. So much so that Hiram, King of Tyre, sent workers to build David a house. A house that we will see later becomes a source of pride and is the root of his drifting away from God.

## Inside the House of David

10 And David went on, and grew great, and the LORD God of hosts was with him.

11 And Hiram king of Tyre sent messengers to David, and cedar trees, and carpenters, and masons: and they built David an house.

12 And David perceived that the LORD had established him king over Israel, and that he had exalted his kingdom for his people Israel's sake.

13 And David took him more concubines and wives out of Jerusalem, after he was come from Hebron: and there were yet sons and daughters born to David.

14 And these be the names of those that were born unto him in Jerusalem; Shammua, and Shobab, and Nathan, and Solomon,

15 Ibhar also, and Elishua, and Nepheg, and Japhia,

16 And Elishama, and Eliada, and Eliphalet.

17 But when the Philistines heard that they had anointed David king over Israel, all the Philistines came up to seek David; and David heard of it, and went down to the hold.

18 The Philistines also came and spread themselves in the valley of Rephaim.

19 And David enquired of the LORD, saying, Shall I go up to the Philistines? wilt thou deliver them into mine hand? And the LORD said unto David, Go up: for I will doubtless deliver the Philistines into thine hand.

20 And David came to Baalperazim, and David smote them there, and said, The LORD hath broken forth upon mine enemies before me, as the breach of waters. Therefore he called the name of that place Baalperazim.

21 And there they left their images, and David and his men burned them.

## The United Kingdom

David's family continues to grow as he takes on even more wives and concubines. Here the Bible names eleven more sons, including Solomon, who will be born to David in Jerusalem.

Another people also heard of David and his capture of Jerusalem, but their reaction was quite different from that of Hiram, King of Tyre. The Philistines sent an army instead of workers. The purpose of the army was to destroy the house of David, not build it. What was David's reaction? Most of us would march out against the enemy and ask God to help us. David does what a man after God's own heart would do - he first asks God what he should do.

### A Man After God's Own Heart

**A man after God's own heart will ask God's direction BEFORE he takes action.**

Do you want to be a man after God's own heart? Then ask God for his guidance before you act or react. I had a very wise preacher tell me one time that is easy to act like a Christian, but hard to react like one. The truth of that statement is enormous.

Not only did David ask God if he should go out and face the enemy, but he also asked him if he would deliver them into his hands? God answered in the affirmative on both counts. If our confidence is in God, then our confidence should be supreme.

### A Man After God's Own Heart

**Another indication if you're a man after God's own heart is what do you do when the victory is won? David gave God the glory and burned their gods.**

How often do we take the glory and spoils for ourselves? Often we rob God of the glory and don't even realize we're doing it.

I was at a gas station once and a man asked me if I could give him a jump since his van wouldn't start. Being a good Christian, I said I'd be happy to and helped him get his van started. He thanked me and I said, "You're welcome." As he drove off it occurred to me that I had just sinned without even realizing it. If it surprised you that I said

I had just sinned, then perhaps you're robbing God of the glory and that you haven't been aware of it, either.

How did I rob God of the glory, you ask? As far as that man knew I was just a nice guy, which made me look good and therefore, gave me the glory. Meaning, I had to think of a way for God to receive the glory and not me. The Bible says in Mark 9:41, *"For whosoever shall give you a cup of water in my name, because you belong to Christ, verily I say unto you he shall not lose his reward."*

So now when I do a good deed and someone thanks me, I simply say, "It was the Christian thing to do." You can say whatever you like, but just be sure the person knows you did it for Christ's sake, and not because you're such a good person. I confess, it's still not easy to do because it's so much easier just to say thank you, but if you're a man after God's own heart and you truly put God first, you will give him the glory.

*22 And the Philistines came up yet again, and spread themselves in the valley of Rephaim.*

*23 And when David enquired of the LORD, he said, Thou shalt not go up; but fetch a compass behind them, and come upon them over against the mulberry trees.*

*24 And let it be, when thou hearest the sound of a going in the tops of the mulberry trees, that then thou shalt bestir thyself: for then shall the LORD go out before thee, to smite the host of the Philistines.*

*25 And David did so, as the LORD had commanded him; and smote the Philistines from Geba until thou come to Gazer.*

The enemy has been defeated and now David's problems are over, right? No, because the enemies of God keep coming back. The Philistines again return, and they go right back to where they were before. Only this time I'm sure they're better prepared to face David and his army.

Here is another opportunity to see if you're a man after God's own heart. How often do we face an enemy we've faced before and defeated, to only have to face them again? If we're not relying on God we'll face them the same way we did the first time. After all, it worked once so it should work again.

Notice that David didn't presume to know the will of God just because he had been in an almost identical situation. Instead of marching out to face the Philistines and assume God was with him just like He had been the first time, David once again asks God what he should do.

### A Man After God's Own Heart

**A man after God's own heart doesn't presume to know the will of God before he asks, even in matters where we think we know what to do because of past experience. The Christian walk is not walk of experience; it's a spiritual walk where we rely on God no matter our past experiences.**

It's a good thing David asked God what he should do, because God had him do something different. No doubt the Philistines were prepared to face David as they did the first time, but this time they would be ready for him. Instead, God told him to circle around behind them and wait for the signal – the rustling of a breeze in the leaves of the Mulberry trees.

To hear the rustling of leaves by the presence of a breeze, we have to be silent and patient. Notice that God didn't use a clap of thunder, or a mighty whirlwind; he used a gentle breeze. Perhaps it was God's way of calming the heart of David before the battle by having him wait patiently in silence until the moment God said to attack. To me that's a sign of a loving God. David was a great warrior and king not because of his supreme self-confidence, but because of his confidence in the supreme God.

# Chapter 6

## The Ark of God

David gathers his army, but this time it's not to go out to battle; it's to retrieve the Ark of God. Why gather an army to bring something as simple as the ark back, when all that was needed was an ox cart? We protect what we cherish, and the fact that David brought an army is an indication of just how precious the ark was. This wasn't just a piece of furniture; it was the ark of God!

If you have ever seen the movie, "Raiders of the Lost Ark," you have seen an accurate recreation of its appearance in the way it looked. However, unlike the movie's premise, the power of the ark lay not in the ark, but in God. What was the purpose of the ark? I believe the purpose of the ark was to help the Israelites focus on God. We often hear how God is omnipresent, which means He's everywhere at all times. How do you focus on a God who is everywhere? Since God is of such great magnitude in all things, we as humans have a hard time trying to understand a God of such magnitude. So much so that we really cannot understand everything about God, because if we could, we would have to be God. So, God gave Israel the Ark so they could more easily focus on Him.

During Old Testament times the Word of God had not yet been completed. The same was true even during the times of King David when much of the Old Testament had yet to be completed. So, God gave His people an object on which to focus their attention when they wanted to meet with Him. Remember, in Old Testament times the Holy Spirit had not yet been given, God had not yet been fully revealed to people and unlike today, the only way to enter into the presence of God was to be the High Priest on one day a year. We no longer need an object such as the Ark of the Covenant because we have the completed Word of God. We have the Spirit of God within us to reveal God through his Word and we can enter into his presence simply through prayer.

We make movies about the Ark of the Covenant and marvel at its power, yet we have a much more powerful tool of God in our homes, but we fail to use it or harness its power. Our Bible contains more than the ten commandments, rod of Aaron and a bowl of manna. Our Bible contains the completed Word of God. It contains everything we need to live a Christian life of abundance. However, just like the power of the ark lay not in the ark, but in the God of the ark; the power of the Bible lies not in the Bible, but in the God of the Bible. That is why it is so important to study the Word of God so He may continue to reveal Himself to us!

## *II Samuel Chapter VI*

*1 Again, David gathered together all the chosen men of Israel, thirty thousand.*

*2 And David arose, and went with all the people that were with him from Baale of Judah, to bring up from thence the ark of God, whose name is called by the name of the LORD of hosts that dwelleth between the cherubims.*

*3 And they set the ark of God upon a new cart, and brought it out of the house of Abinadab that was in Gibeah: and Uzzah and Ahio, the sons of Abinadab, drave the new cart.*

*4 And they brought it out of the house of Abinadab which was at Gibeah, accompanying the ark of God: and Ahio went before the ark.*

*5 And David and all the house of Israel played before the LORD on all manner of instruments made of fir wood, even on harps, and on psalteries, and on timbrels, and on cornets, and on cymbals.*

## The Ark of God

*6 And when they came to Nachon's threshingfloor, Uzzah put forth his hand to the ark of God, and took hold of it; for the oxen shook it.*

*7 And the anger of the LORD was kindled against Uzzah; and God smote him there for his error; and there he died by the ark of God.*

The ark was in the house of Abinadab, where it had been since before Samuel had anointed Saul as the first king over Israel. *1 "And the men of Kirjathjearim came, and fetched up the ark of the LORD, and brought it into the house of Abinadab in the hill, and sanctified Eleazar his son to keep the ark of the LORD. 2 And it came to pass, while the ark abode in Kirjathjearim, that the time was long; for it was twenty years: and all the house of Israel lamented after the LORD."* (I Samuel 7:1-2). Two of Abinadab's son's drove the ox cart, Uzzah and Ahio. Uzzah drove the cart while Ahio walked ahead with the oxen.

As the cart drove along toward Jerusalem, David and all of Israel celebrated by dancing and playing music on various instruments. This was a parade with the Ark of God as its focal point. That is, until Uzzah who had switched places with Ahio, made himself the focal point by appearing to assist God in steadying the ark. What was wrong with Uzzah doing something as innocent as trying to steady the ark so it wouldn't fall off the cart? Simply put, if Uzzah was really innocent, then God wouldn't have been angered.

So what was Uzzah guilty of? Imagine if you were driving the cart carrying the Ark of God, with the king and all Israel dancing around the cart you were driving. That could make a man proud. So proud in fact that the man felt a desire to bring even more of a focus on himself by showing everyone that he was the one that kept the ark safe.

Was the ark in danger of falling? I would strongly suggest it wasn't in any danger. Is God not big enough to steady His own ark? Uzzah was presuming on God, and he did it by calling attention to himself and not God. God wants the attention, not because of a character flaw, but because he's the only way to an abundant life, but more importantly, salvation.

Uzzah's punishment for stealing God's glory was death. This put a somber and fearful tone onto what had been a joyous celebration. David didn't know quite what to do, because he too was afraid. Outwardly, no one could see what Uzzah did wrong, but God looks on the heart.

*8 And David was displeased, because the LORD had made a breach upon Uzzah: and he called the name of the place Perezuzzah to this day.*

*9 And David was afraid of the LORD that day, and said, How shall the ark of the LORD come to me?*

*10 So David would not remove the ark of the LORD unto him into the city of David: but David carried it aside into the house of Obededom the Gittite.*

*11 And the ark of the LORD continued in the house of Obededom the Gittite three months: and the LORD blessed Obededom, and all his household.*

*12 And it was told king David, saying, The LORD hath blessed the house of Obededom, and all that pertaineth unto him, because of the ark of God. So David went and brought up the ark of God from the house of Obededom into the city of David with gladness.*

*13 And it was so, that when they that bare the ark of the LORD had gone six paces, he sacrificed oxen and fatlings.*

*14 And David danced before the LORD with all his might; and David was girded with a linen ephod.*

*15 So David and all the house of Israel brought up the ark of the LORD with shouting, and with the sound of the trumpet.*

*16 And as the ark of the LORD came into the city of David, Michal Saul's daughter looked through a window, and saw king David leaping and dancing before the LORD; and she despised him in her heart.*

## The Ark of God

*17 And they brought in the ark of the LORD, and set it in his place, in the midst of the tabernacle that David had pitched for it: and David offered burnt offerings and peace offerings before the LORD.*

*18 And as soon as David had made an end of offering burnt offerings and peace offerings, he blessed the people in the name of the LORD of hosts.*

*19 And he dealt among all the people, even among the whole multitude of Israel, as well to the women as men, to every one a cake of bread, and a good piece of flesh, and a flagon of wine. So all the people departed every one to his house.*

*20 Then David returned to bless his household. And Michal the daughter of Saul came out to meet David, and said, How glorious was the king of Israel to day, who uncovered himself to day in the eyes of the handmaids of his servants, as one of the vain fellows shamelessly uncovereth himself!*

*21 And David said unto Michal, It was before the LORD, which chose me before thy father, and before all his house, to appoint me ruler over the people of the LORD, over Israel: therefore will I play before the LORD.*

*22 And I will yet be more vile than thus, and will be base in mine own sight: and of the maidservants which thou hast spoken of, of them shall I be had in honour.*

*23 Therefore Michal the daughter of Saul had no child unto the day of her death.*

The Bible says in verse 8 that David was displeased because the Lord had made a breach upon Uzzah. Does this mean David was mad at God? No, I don't think so, and the reason I don't think so is because David knew God was just. God is all-knowing. God is all-loving. God is all-just. To be angry at a God like that would be very foolish, because if we did get angry with God, we would be setting up our self as knowing more than God, loving more than God, and being more just than God. That is being Presumptuous with a capital "P."

David feared God, not as a child fears a monster, but as young man fears his father because of his respect for that father. He wasn't sure how to proceed with the ark because he wasn't sure if God was still angry, or angry at Israel for an unknown reason. So, he appears to have taken it to the nearest house, which belonged to Obed-edom, the Gittite. I wonder what Obed thought to have the ark of God in his house. They had just witnessed the power of God, so I'm sure they were very cautious around the ark. Not just physically careful, but more importantly, spiritually.

For three months the ark stayed in the house of Obed-edom, and in that time God blessed his house. Was Obed-edom and his family perfect during that time? No, but their heart was right because it wasn't presumptuous, it was respectful. When David learned that Obed's house had been blessed, he knew that God was no longer angry, and he could finish the job he started at the beginning of the chapter.

The ark was taken to Jerusalem among much fanfare and celebrating. Also, this time, David transported the ark as God originally commanded, being carried by the priests and not in an ox cart. After going only six paces, as if to not take any chances, they stopped and offered an offering to God. David then danced clothed only with a linen ephod. When they entered the city, Michal, David's wife who was also the daughter of Saul, saw him and the Bible says she despised him in her heart.

What had David done wrong? In verse 20 she tells him that he danced shamelessly uncovered so that all the women could lust after him. Was she jealous? It seems to me the Bible answers that question, first in verse 16 when it describes Michal as the daughter of Saul, and not as the wife of David. Then in verse 21 when David answers her accusation he seems to think her anger is rooted in the fact that he is the king and not her father. Remember, Michal's father and all her brothers are dead, or the ones who haven't been killed were sons of concubines and therefore not eligible for the throne.

Family ties are hard to break, even if it's a wife needing to break ties with her family to follow her husband. It seems that as the years passed, Michal began to resent David because he had become king and her own father, the former king was dead. Of course, David in no uncertain terms reminds her that God chose him to be king, and not Saul, her father.

David could have handled the situation much better, but instead he chose to defend his actions by telling Michal that if he wanted all those handmaids she talked about, he could have them and they'd be happy. He was saying, if you don't like me there are plenty of others who will. He lived up to that threat, if you want to call it that, because he eventually married 300 women and had 400 concubines - a bit of overkill if you ask me.

It also seems David could carry a grudge, because Michal would not have any children. I'm not sure if she was barren, or if David simply never went in to be intimate with her so she could have a child.

Another note about this chapter before we leave it. The day had been a glorious day, and everyone had been fed that day and all had been very festive. The Ark of God was in its rightful place and apparently all was well. Maybe that's why David reacted as he did toward Michal. She should have been happy too on this day, but instead she was selfish in that she tried to make something bad out of something good. Michal had let her emotions interfere with a festive occasion, and the price was steep, as it often is when we allow our emotions to dictate to our reason, resulting in dangerous actions.

# Chapter 7

## The Davidic Covenant

*II Samuel Chapter VII*

*1 And it came to pass, when the king sat in his house, and the LORD had given him rest round about from all his enemies;*

*2 That the king said unto Nathan the prophet, See now, I dwell in an house of cedar, but the ark of God dwelleth within curtains.*

*3 And Nathan said to the king, Go, do all that is in thine heart; for the LORD is with thee.*

*4 And it came to pass that night, that the word of the LORD came unto Nathan, saying,*

*5 Go and tell my servant David, Thus saith the LORD, Shalt thou build me an house for me to dwell in?*

*6 Whereas I have not dwelt in any house since the time that I brought up the children of Israel out of Egypt, even to this day, but have walked in a tent and in a tabernacle.*

*7 In all the places wherein I have walked with all the children of Israel spake I a word with any of the tribes of Israel, whom I commanded to feed my people Israel, saying, Why build ye not me an house of cedar?*

*8 Now therefore so shalt thou say unto my servant David, Thus saith the LORD of hosts, I took thee from the sheepcote, from following the sheep, to be ruler over my people, over Israel:*

*9 And I was with thee whithersoever thou wentest, and have cut off all thine enemies out of thy sight, and have made thee a great name, like unto the name of the great men that are in the earth.*

*10 Moreover I will appoint a place for my people Israel, and will plant them, that they may dwell in a place of their own, and move no more; neither shall the children of wickedness afflict them any more, as beforetime,*

*11 And as since the time that I commanded judges to be over my people Israel, and have caused thee to rest from all thine enemies. Also the LORD telleth thee that he will make thee an house.*

*12 And when thy days be fulfilled, and thou shalt sleep with thy fathers, I will set up thy seed after thee, which shall proceed out of thy bowels, and I will establish his kingdom.*

*13 He shall build an house for my name, and I will stablish the throne of his kingdom for ever.*

*14 I will be his father, and he shall be my son. If he commit iniquity, I will chasten him with the rod of men, and with the stripes of the children of men:*

*15 But my mercy shall not depart away from him, as I took it from Saul, whom I put away before thee.*

*16 And thine house and thy kingdom shall be established for ever before thee: thy throne shall be established for ever.*

*17 According to all these words, and according to all this vision, so did Nathan speak unto David.*

We next find King David sitting in his house because God had given him rest from his enemies. This gave David time to think, and also time to appreciate what God had given him. However, he's going to appreciate his house a bit too much. As he sits there he tells Nathan, the prophet, that it doesn't seem fair for him to dwell in such a nice house when God was dwelling in a tent.

## The Davidic Covenant

On the surface it would seem that David's heart was in the right place and thinking of God first. Nathan seems to think the same thing and what David says seems reasonable to him, because he tells David to go and do all that is in his heart because God is with him. However, things are not as they seem on the surface. Nathan assumes God had laid it on David's heart to build him a house, but God did no such thing (Notice Nathan failed to ask God's direction before he advised David). Nathan assumed that David was thinking of God when he suggested building God a house, but in reality David was thinking of David.

What was David's motive for building God a house? We will see it wasn't because God laid it on his heart. David was feeling guilty because his possessions, namely his house, were replacing his love for God. David sensed it, but didn't want to face it, so instead of repenting, he sought to cover up what was becoming his sin by doing something to honor God, and at the same time, appease him. However, God doesn't ask us to appease him, he asks us to love, trust and obey Him.

Most religions are about appeasing God. They say you have to be good to get to heaven, as if our righteousness is enough to satisfy God. God says our righteousness is as filthy rags (Isaiah 64:6). God also says that if our motive for serving Him is to be based on love (I Cor. 3:13-15 and chapter 13).

We may fool others, as David did Nathan. We may try to fool ourselves, as David tried by seeking to assuage his guilt by offering to build God a fine house too. However, we can never fool God because God looks on the heart and he knows the motivation for our actions. Even if those actions on the surface appear to be God honoring.

So God comes to Nathan that night and gives him a message for David. God's message begins by asking David why he wants to build Him a house. He then goes on to say He hasn't had one since he brought Israel out of Egypt. He says that He's never asked anyone or even any tribe to build Him a house. Notice in verse 7, God specifies the house David wants to build as a house of cedar, just like

David's house. That statement in itself should have struck home with David, since it was focusing in on the thoughts of his heart.

Then in verse 8 God goes on to speak directly to David. He is reminding David of what He has done for him. He took him from being a shepherd, to ruling over all His people of Israel. It was God who defeated David's enemies and made him great. He will establish His people. By saying "He will," he is saying, I've not done it yet, but I will do it." The point being that God will do it. Not David, but God.

In verse 11 God reminds David that even his house is a gift from God. However, David won't be the one to build God a house, that job will fall to his son. He will establish David's throne and it will be established forever. David's throne does go on throughout history until Jesus, the Messiah, takes his place on that throne. When Jesus died on the cross, then rose again, he fulfilled that promise because he is the last of David's decedents that ever needs to sit on the throne, because being God, Jesus is eternal.

*18 Then went king David in, and sat before the LORD, and he said, Who am I, O Lord GOD? and what is my house, that thou hast brought me hitherto?*

*19 And this was yet a small thing in thy sight, O Lord GOD; but thou hast spoken also of thy servant's house for a great while to come. And is this the manner of man, O Lord GOD?*

*20 And what can David say more unto thee? for thou, Lord GOD, knowest thy servant.*

*21 For thy word's sake, and according to thine own heart, hast thou done all these great things, to make thy servant know them.*

*22 Wherefore thou art great, O LORD God: for there is none like thee, neither is there any God beside thee, according to all that we have heard with our ears.*

*23 And what one nation in the earth is like thy people, even like Israel, whom God went to redeem for a people to himself, and to*

## The Davidic Covenant

*make him a name, and to do for you great things and terrible, for thy land, before thy people, which thou redeemedst to thee from Egypt, from the nations and their gods?*

*24 For thou hast confirmed to thyself thy people Israel to be a people unto thee for ever: and thou, LORD, art become their God.*

*25 And now, O LORD God, the word that thou hast spoken concerning thy servant, and concerning his house, establish it for ever, and do as thou hast said.*

*26 And let thy name be magnified for ever, saying, The LORD of hosts is the God over Israel: and let the house of thy servant David be established before thee.*

*27 For thou, O LORD of hosts, God of Israel, hast revealed to thy servant, saying, I will build thee an house: therefore hath thy servant found in his heart to pray this prayer unto thee.*

*28 And now, O Lord GOD, thou art that God, and thy words be true, and thou hast promised this goodness unto thy servant:*

*29 Therefore now let it please thee to bless the house of thy servant, that it may continue for ever before thee: for thou, O Lord GOD, hast spoken it: and with thy blessing let the house of thy servant be blessed for ever.*

Verse 18 begins David's response to God through his prayer. He asks two questions, "Who am I," and, "What is my house, that thou hast brought me hitherto?" David is in wonderment that God would be so good to him, because he knows he doesn't deserve God's goodness.

David recognized that God was doing all this for him, not because of his own goodness, but because, as he says in verse 21, *"For thy words sake, and according to thine own heart..."*

As a result of God's goodness, David starts praising God. He thanks Him for the nation of Israel also, praising Him for his goodness toward the Israelites.

## A Man After God's Own Heart

**Another way that David showed himself to be a man after God's own heart was his gratitude for what God was doing in his life. He considered himself a servant of God and as a servant he was willing to do whatever it is God required of him.**

Of course, it was easy to be God's servant when good things resulted. However, that house, that house of David's would come back to haunt him, because it was love for his house which began the slide away from God, which led to Bathsheba.

# Chapter 8

## Peace in the Kingdom

*II Samuel Chapter VIII*

*1 And after this it came to pass, that David smote the Philistines, and subdued them: and David took Methegammah out of the hand of the Philistines.*

*2 And he smote Moab, and measured them with a line, casting them down to the ground; even with two lines measured he to put to death, and with one full line to keep alive. And so the Moabites became David's servants, and brought gifts.*

*3 David smote also Hadadezer, the son of Rehob, king of Zobah, as he went to recover his border at the river Euphrates.*

*4 And David took from him a thousand chariots, and seven hundred horsemen, and twenty thousand footmen: and David houghed all the chariot horses, but reserved of them for an hundred chariots.*

*5 And when the Syrians of Damascus came to succour Hadadezer king of Zobah, David slew of the Syrians two and twenty thousand men.*

*6 Then David put garrisons in Syria of Damascus: and the Syrians became servants to David, and brought gifts. And the LORD preserved David whithersoever he went.*

*7 And David took the shields of gold that were on the servants of Hadadezer, and brought them to Jerusalem.*

*8 And from Betah, and from Berothai, cities of Hadadezer, king David took exceeding much brass.*

*9 When Toi king of Hamath heard that David had smitten all the host of Hadadezer,*

*10 Then Toi sent Joram his son unto king David, to salute him, and to bless him, because he had fought against Hadadezer, and smitten him: for Hadadezer had wars with Toi. And Joram brought with him vessels of silver, and vessels of gold, and vessels of brass:*

*11 Which also king David did dedicate unto the LORD, with the silver and gold that he had dedicated of all nations which he subdued;*

*12 Of Syria, and of Moab, and of the children of Ammon, and of the Philistines, and of Amalek, and of the spoil of Hadadezer, son of Rehob, king of Zobah.*

*13 And David gat him a name when he returned from smiting of the Syrians in the valley of salt, being eighteen thousand men.*

*14 And he put garrisons in Edom; throughout all Edom put he garrisons, and all they of Edom became David's servants. And the LORD preserved David whithersoever he went.*

*15 And David reigned over all Israel; and David executed judgment and justice unto all his people.*

*16 And Joab the son of Zeruiah was over the host; and Jehoshaphat the son of Ahilud was recorder;*

*17 And Zadok the son of Ahitub, and Ahimelech the son of Abiathar, were the priests; and Seraiah was the scribe;*

*18 And Benaiah the son of Jehoiada was over both the Cherethites and the Pelethites; and David's sons were chief rulers.*

Chapter 8 is a military history of the exploits of King David; the greatest of the Kings of Israel and the king who captured more territory than any king before or since. The Philistines were the first people that David subdued. The Philistines were in what we know today as the Gaza Strip. The next nation that David subdues is Moab, which is east of the Dead Sea and is now part of western Jordan. King David took away the fighting strength of Moab when Israel executed about half its army. Today we may see that as an atrocity, but in what we call ancient history, it was a common practice. Today people talk about disarmament, in David's day most practiced "dissoldierment." After all, it was war that was being fought, and the rules of war are set by the victors.

Next David marched his army toward the River Euphrates, but between him and the river was Zobah, and her king, Hadadezer. Zobah was located in present day Syria between Damascus and the Euphrates River. Verse 3 says David went to recover his border at the Euphrates. Since Israel had never had that territory in her national history, how could David "recover" it? Israel had never occupied that territory, but it was given to Israel by God, and so David was claiming what was given to his nation by the God of the universe in Genesis 15:18, *"In the same day the LORD made a covenant with Abram, saying, Unto thy seed have I given this land, from the river of Egypt unto the great river, the river Euphrates:"* This wasn't a one-time gift or promise that was later withdrawn, but it was an everlasting covenant (Gen. 17:8). *"And I will give unto thee, and to thy seed after thee, the land wherein thou art a stranger, all the land of Canaan, for an everlasting possession; and I will be their God."* How long is everlasting? The territory that was given by God to Israel is now being claimed, or as God termed it here in II Samuel, recovered.

Hadadezer was defeated and the spoils of war yielded David a thousand chariots, with their horses, which he disabled to prevent them from being used against him in the future. However, he held one hundred back to include in his own army.

David had done three thousand years ago what the United States was to do in WWII in the Pacific through "island hopping," which was the practice of passing by fortified islands forcing the Japanese to evacuate. David had gone around Damascus to reach Zobah, and now that Zobah had been defeated, Damascus was isolated as the Japanese held islands had been during WWII. So, the Syrian army marches to try and rescue Hadadezer from David's army only to be defeated themselves and lose 22,000 men in the process. This put David over Syria and they paid tribute as David placed garrisons in Syria to protect what he had gained.

God preserved David or protected him wherever he went. Through all the trials and circumstances in David's life, God had prepared him to accomplish the goals God set for him. In the process of accomplishing those goals, God also protected him.

Verses 8-12 tell of the spoils of war which fell into David's hands: Some through conquest, some through tribute, and some through a showing of respect. What did David do with these riches? He dedicated them to God.

### A Man After God's Own Heart

**David understood that all he had belonged to God; therefore, he dedicated all he had to God. When we understand that it all belongs to God, we don't become selfish or prideful, but use what He gives us to bring glory to Him.**

Our money and belongings do not belong to us, they belong to God. Dedicate what you have to God. That doesn't mean you give it all away to a church, but it does mean you use it in a way that will bring honor to God and for righteous works.

Verse 13 says David gat him a name. His fame started to spread throughout the region, which meant he was feared of those that may lay in his path and that he was someone that needed to be dealt with. Some chose war, some chose tribute, and some chose to honor and respect him. At one time David had been abased and in fear for his life as he fled from before Saul. He had faked being mad in Gath on one those occasions, but now he commanded respect as he did what God would have him do. Remember, the times of trials are what prepared him to be the great king he became. Just as your trials are preparing you for what God wants you to become.

Edom, which today would be southern Jordan, also came under David's control as he placed garrisons in the land. The rest of the chapter tells us who David's men were who helped him manage this empire God was using him to create. No man does it alone. to achieve great things for God, put him first and seek after righteousness, and find people to help you in your work to bring honor and glory to Him. After all, we give glory to God because it's only through Him we can be saved.

# Chapter 9

## For the Love of Jonathan

*II Samuel Chapter IX*

*1 And David said, Is there yet any that is left of the house of Saul, that I may shew him kindness for Jonathan's sake?*

*2 And there was of the house of Saul a servant whose name was Ziba. And when they had called him unto David, the king said unto him, Art thou Ziba? And he said, Thy servant is he.*

*3 And the king said, Is there not yet any of the house of Saul, that I may shew the kindness of God unto him? And Ziba said unto the king, Jonathan hath yet a son, which is lame on his feet.*

*4 And the king said unto him, Where is he? And Ziba said unto the king, Behold, he is in the house of Machir, the son of Ammiel, in Lodebar.*

*5 Then king David sent, and fetched him out of the house of Machir, the son of Ammiel, from Lodebar.*

It appears David may have been sitting on his throne and contemplating his past in a nostalgic way. When we do the same, we often think of people who used to be in our lives that made an impact and we naturally miss them. A person David knew and missed was a man he loved as a friend by the name of Jonathan, who also happened to be the son of the man who had sought to kill David, Saul.

Jonathan had been killed in the same battle as his father Saul, and however long it was later, David is recalling his best friend and the promise he made to show kindness to his house should anything happen to Jonathan (I Samuel 20:14-17). In this time of reflection, David remembered his covenant with Jonathan and hoped for an opportunity to fulfill it by being kind to someone from Jonathan's family.

The first verse begins when David asks, *"Is there yet any that is left of the house of Saul, that I may show him kindness for Jonathan's sake?"* In the age of kings, it was common practice for kings to slay any, what was called, pretenders to the throne. For that reason, the families of former kings were often killed. At one time Saul was angry enough with Jonathan to have had him killed, and he even ordered it so (I Samuel 14:44-45) but the people rescued Jonathan from his father, the king.

Matthew 2:8 gives us an example of a king asking to be told where someone was so that he might come and worship him. Herod was seeking to destroy the legitimate heir to the throne of David, whereas David was seeking to honor the memory of his friend Jonathan, through Mephibosheth, his son, who had been heir to the throne of Saul. God had taken the right to rule from Saul and his posterity and given it to David and his posterity, meaning that David was the rightful king of Israel as Mephibosheth could never be. Some may think that what David was asking was nothing more than a trick to kill any possible pretender to the throne. There will always be people who jump to false conclusions because of their own negative personality.

David was sincere in his request to show kindness to the house of Saul. Notice also that it wasn't just the house of Jonathan, but the entire house of Saul. David had reason to hate Saul for all the trouble he caused him, but he always respected Saul as God's anointed.

### A Man After God's Own Heart

**David's love for God first, then his love for Saul's son Jonathan, overcame any animosity he may have felt toward Saul. David was a**

man after God's own heart because he allowed love to overcome possible bitterness. So how do we overcome people who use us and mistreat us? The answer to that question may be found in Matthew 5:44, *"But I say unto you, Love your enemies, bless them that curse you, do good to them that hate you, and pray for them which despitefully use you, and persecute you;"*

*6 Now when Mephibosheth, the son of Jonathan, the son of Saul, was come unto David, he fell on his face, and did reverence. And David said, Mephibosheth. And he answered, Behold thy servant!*

*7 And David said unto him, Fear not: for I will surely shew thee kindness for Jonathan thy father's sake, and will restore thee all the land of Saul thy father; and thou shalt eat bread at my table continually.*

*8 And he bowed himself, and said, What is thy servant, that thou shouldest look upon such a dead dog as I am?*

*9 Then the king called to Ziba, Saul's servant, and said unto him, I have given unto thy master's son all that pertained to Saul and to all his house.*

*10 Thou therefore, and thy sons, and thy servants, shall till the land for him, and thou shalt bring in the fruits, that thy master's son may have food to eat: but Mephibosheth thy master's son shall eat bread alway at my table. Now Ziba had fifteen sons and twenty servants.*

*11 Then said Ziba unto the king, According to all that my lord the king hath commanded his servant, so shall thy servant do. As for Mephibosheth, said the king, he shall eat at my table, as one of the king's sons.*

*12 And Mephibosheth had a young son, whose name was Micha. And all that dwelt in the house of Ziba were servants unto Mephibosheth.*

*13 So Mephibosheth dwelt in Jerusalem: for he did eat continually at the king's table; and was lame on both his feet.*

Apparently, to please the king, a search was made to find an answer to the king's question. Ziba, a former servant of Saul's house was located and brought before the king. David asked him the question and Ziba's answer must have pleased David, because he found that a son of Jonathan was yet living. David asked where he was specifically, and Ziba told him the house in which he could be found. So, David sent for him.

I wonder what was going through Mephibosheth's mind when he was told he had to appear before the king? When he entered the court of King David he fell on his face and did reverence. How do we come before our King, the King of Kings? Do we come to God with respect, or are we flippant toward the creator? Is God, God, or is he "the man upstairs?"

As Mephibosheth lay with his face toward the ground David said his name and he answered by saying, *"Behold thy servant?"* He made no claim to the throne of his father. He didn't allow a false pride to make him figuratively stand defiantly before the king. He humbled himself as he should have done before God's anointed.

What would have happened if Mephibosheth hadn't humbled himself? David had sworn to protect Jonathan's family, so it would follow that David would have protected Mephibosheth, even from himself. Mephibosheth wouldn't have had to suffer the fate that would have awaited him if he had publicly defied his king simply because of the covenant made between David and Jonathan.

The first two words David said after Mephibosheth humbled himself was *"Fear not."* How often do we hear those words in scripture? The two words appear together 62 times in the King James Bible. I suspect, though I cannot prove, that when we die, the first two words we hear upon entering heaven are the words, "Fear not."

David goes on to tell Mephibosheth that he will show him kindness, and then he puts weight behind his words by also restoring to him all the lands of his father Saul and tells him he will eat at his table. Mephibosheth is going to eat at the king's table and inherit his father's land, not for what he did, but for the sake of what Jonathan had done. Conversely, we will inherit of our Heavenly Father and eat at the King's table in heaven, not for what we have done, but for the sake of Jesus Christ and what he did.

Mephibosheth knew he wasn't worthy, any more than we are worthy of what God gives to those who accept His free gift of salvation. David then called for Ziba and gave him the job of being steward over the inheritance of Mephibosheth. Ziba assured King David that he would do as the king commanded. Mephibosheth had a young son who was also going to benefit for what his Grandfather Jonathan had done years before as David's friend.

# Chapter 10

## The Warrior King

*II Samuel Chapter X*

*1 And it came to pass after this, that the king of the children of Ammon died, and Hanun his son reigned in his stead.*

*2 Then said David, I will shew kindness unto Hanun the son of Nahash, as his father shewed kindness unto me. And David sent to comfort him by the hand of his servants for his father. And David's servants came into the land of the children of Ammon.*

*3 And the princes of the children of Ammon said unto Hanun their lord, Thinkest thou that David doth honour thy father, that he hath sent comforters unto thee? hath not David rather sent his servants unto thee, to search the city, and to spy it out, and to overthrow it?*

*4 Wherefore Hanun took David's servants, and shaved off the one half of their beards, and cut off their garments in the middle, even to their buttocks, and sent them away.*

*5 When they told it unto David, he sent to meet them, because the men were greatly ashamed: and the king said, Tarry at Jericho until your beards be grown, and then return.*

How often do people jump to the wrong conclusion and then later realize their mistake after it's too late? Worse still, how often do you accept bad advice, act on it, and then later regret our decision? Hanun succeeded his father as King of Ammon and by listening and acting on bad advice, he brought the wrath of King David down upon him.

When Hanun's father died, David sent messengers in peace on a goodwill mission to comfort Hanun. Most likely they carried gifts and items of value, as we would do to comfort the family of a friend who had died by cooking them meals. David was showing this kindness because Hanun's father had shown him kindness. However, Hanun's advisers, the princes of Ammon, told their new king it was a trick to spy out the defenses of Ammon so David could attack. On what did they base their evidence? They had no evidence, all they had was fear. They knew David was a mighty king expanding his kingdom, and so they assumed his intention was to overthrow Ammon now that the king he was indebted to had died.

So Hanun ordered that the goodwill ambassadors be taken, half their beards shaved off, their garments cut so that they were exposed to the point of shame, then sent them back to Jerusalem. David, upon hearing what had happened to his ambassadors, sent some of his men to meet them at Jericho in deference to their condition. He showed compassion and understanding, and his anger was kindled.

We are ambassadors of our king. Sometimes when we are in his duty we are mistreated and humiliated through no fault of our own. Hanun punished David's messengers, not because of what they had done, but because of who they represented. These men didn't rail against Hanun and demand their rights. They suffered in silence and David heard what happened, the same way God hears our prayers and shows compassion and understanding. God's anger is also kindled and as the Bible says in Deuteronomy 32:35 and Romans 12:19, *"Dearly beloved, avenge not yourselves, but rather give place unto wrath: for it is written, Vengeance is mine; I will repay, saith the Lord."* David's men did not seek revenge; they left that up to their king, who had the power to repay in much greater proportion, just as God has the power to repay for the wrongs done to us in a much greater proportion.

*6 And when the children of Ammon saw that they stank before David, the children of Ammon sent and hired the Syrians of Bethrehob, and the Syrians of Zoba, twenty thousand footmen, and of king Maacah a thousand men, and of Ishtob twelve thousand men.*

## The Warrior King

7 And when David heard of it, he sent Joab, and all the host of the mighty men.

8 And the children of Ammon came out, and put the battle in array at the entering in of the gate: and the Syrians of Zoba, and of Rehob, and Ishtob, and Maacah, were by themselves in the field.

9 When Joab saw that the front of the battle was against him before and behind, he chose of all the choice men of Israel, and put them in array against the Syrians:

10 And the rest of the people he delivered into the hand of Abishai his brother, that he might put them in array against the children of Ammon.

11 And he said, If the Syrians be too strong for me, then thou shalt help me: but if the children of Ammon be too strong for thee, then I will come and help thee.

12 Be of good courage, and let us play the men for our people, and for the cities of our God: and the LORD do that which seemeth him good.

13 And Joab drew nigh, and the people that were with him, unto the battle against the Syrians: and they fled before him.

14 And when the children of Ammon saw that the Syrians were fled, then fled they also before Abishai, and entered into the city. So Joab returned from the children of Ammon, and came to Jerusalem.

15 And when the Syrians saw that they were smitten before Israel, they gathered themselves together.

16 And Hadarezer sent, and brought out the Syrians that were beyond the river: and they came to Helam; and Shobach the captain of the host of Hadarezer went before them.

17 And when it was told David, he gathered all Israel together, and passed over Jordan, and came to Helam. And the Syrians set themselves in array against David, and fought with him.

*18 And the Syrians fled before Israel; and David slew the men of seven hundred chariots of the Syrians, and forty thousand horsemen, and smote Shobach the captain of their host, who died there.*

*19 And when all the kings that were servants to Hadarezer saw that they were smitten before Israel, they made peace with Israel, and served them. So the Syrians feared to help the children of Ammon any more.*

The spirit of fear present in Ammon now becomes greater because they have provoked King David. Therefore, they call to Syria for help and hired 33,000 men. Ammon was mobilizing and preparing for war. David did not act rashly, because he waited to see what Ammon was going to do. When they hired 33,000 men, he knew they were preparing for war, so David took the war to them. He sent Joab with his army to meet the army of Ammon and the mercenaries they had hired.

Ammon's men came out from the city to meet the Israeli army at the gate, and the Syrians were already positioned outside the city so that if Joab attacked the Ammonites, then he would be in a precarious position with the Ammonites on one side and the Syrians on the other. So, Joab split his army and placed half to fight the Syrians, while the other half was put under command of his brother Abishai to fight the Ammonites. The plan was for the other to assist the one who was having the most difficult fight. What would have happened if they both were losing didn't seem to occur to them. Instead of the spirit of fear, such as what had enveloped the Ammonites, they had the spirit of hope.

This spirit of hope was possible because of what Joab says in verse 12. This is the same spirit of hope that is available to each and every Christian that chooses to exercise faith over fear. *"Be of good courage, and let us play the men for our people, and for the cities of our God: and the Lord do that which seemeth him good."*

We fight for right, motivated by that which we love and hold dear, and leave the outcome to God.

With this spirit of hope Joab takes his half of the army and engages the Syrians who flee before him. Upon seeing the Syrians flee, the Ammonites were overcome by the spirit of fear and return to the safety of their city walls instead of facing the other half of the army led by Abishai.

The army of Israel, having won the victory and without an army to face, returns to Jerusalem. The Syrians regroup with the river between them and David, who has taken over command of the army. David then marches his men over the Jordan River to face the Syrians who attack as he approaches. King David wins the victory, and the Syrians sue for peace and come under the control of Israel. The Syrians feared to help the Ammonites ever again because of the loss they suffered. The spirit of fear had also gripped them, and they surrendered. A Christian should never give up because the spirit we are to have in us is the spirit of hope through our faith in our all-powerful God. Those without God have no such hope and one day their self-confidence will be turned into fear.

# Chapter 11

## The Edge of Darkness

Chapter 11 is one of the most well-known stories of the Bible and a favorite source for preachers who use this chapter to warn of sin. After all, how could a man after God's own heart commit such heinous sins against God and his own people? From my perspective, that shouldn't be such a puzzling question because all of us are capable of sinning to degrees we would vehemently deny in public. Knowing what you know about yourself, and in the quiet of your own mind, you know the darkness that surrounds the light of God in your life. That's why it's important we remain in the center of the light and not dance around the edge of darkness.

Staying in the light of God is not something that comes from attending church regularly and praying before each meal. Staying in the light of God takes effort and a spiritual awareness of our surroundings. Seldom do we march boldly into darkness; rather we drift away from the center of God to the outer edges of the darkness that surrounds us because we have lost focus of the importance of having God as our focal point. We become that center instead of God, and that's when the drifting toward the darkness takes place.

David didn't wake up one morning in the center of God's light and march boldly into the darkness of sin. He, like the rest of us, drifted away from God as he became, what he thought was his own self-sufficiency.

*II Samuel Chapter XI*

*1 And it came to pass, after the year was expired, at the time when kings go forth to battle, that David sent Joab, and his servants with him, and all Israel; and they destroyed the children of Ammon, and besieged Rabbah. But David tarried still at Jerusalem.*

In verse 1 we find David in Jerusalem with his army encamped in the fields as they lay siege to Rabbah. Was David always with his army in the field? The answer is no. II Sam. 10:7 says that David sent Joab and his army to confront Ammon because of King Hanun's ill treatment of the messengers of David. Always before that time David had led the army, but now David stayed home as he sent Joab and entrusted him with leading the army. Here in chapter 11 he does the same thing and stays home while he sends Joab to lead the Israeli army.

Did David sin because he did not take the lead as he always had before? I won't be so bold as to call this sin, but I believe it is safe to say it was one of the signs of David drifting away from the light of God. His duty and his place were with his men. In times past God had blessed him with victories as he led his men in battle. David had become complacent and presumed his armies would be successful because of his past experiences.

When we drift away from God it is usually because our love for God begins being replaced for our love for something other than God. That is the seed of sin and that is why God is a jealous God, because He knows that once our affection is placed on something else besides Him, it leads to our sin and our self-imposed harm, which grieves God.

What then did David love more than God? The answer may surprise you, because most are probably thinking sensual lust because of what happened with Bathsheba. However, Bathsheba was a result of that one thing that David began to love more than God. Are you ready for this? David loved his house more than God.

"His house," you ask? Why do I think that David loved his house more than God? After all, when we compare a house with God, which is greater, and which deserves our love more? God loves us and can show He loves us, but how can a house show love? A house can't show love, so then why did David allow his love for an inanimate object overcome his love for the living God?

First, let's make it clear that David loved his house more than God. Remember from where David came. He had been a shepherd watching over his flocks in the hills. As a shepherd he didn't get to enjoy the pleasures and ease of having a roof over his head and the other comforts a home offers.

When David was sent to live with Saul, he lived in the house of another and I'm sure he was impressed with the comforts of living in a palace. Yet Saul drove him out and for the next seven years David has no home or sanctuary. He lived on the run, in tents, and in caves. The one place where he could temporarily call home, Ziklag, was burned to the ground and David once again moved from place to place. As it says in I Sam. 30:31, *"...and all the places where David himself and his men were wont to haunt."*

David, who had never really known the comforts of a home, longed for one of his own. Maybe he didn't realize it, but we can only covet what we do not have. David coveted Bathsheba, but only after he coveted the comforts of his own home. David's sin would begin in II Sam. 5:11. *"And Hiram king of Tyre sent messengers to David, and cedar trees, and carpenters, and masons: and they built David an house."*

God had blessed David and now David was going to be allowed to live a life of ease. Especially compared to the life he had lived previously as a shepherd and on the run from King Saul. His enemies had been subdued and his victories won. Now was the time for him to enjoy the fruit of his labors.

David admired his house so much; he wanted to build God a house. II Sam. 7:1-2 tells how David thought it improper that God dwelled behind curtains while he dwelled in a house of cedar. He was admiring his house and he felt guilty. So, to assuage his guilt for loving his house, he sought to justify his sin of idolizing his house by his desire to build one for God.

At first Nathan saw nothing wrong with David wanting to build a house for God, after all, what could be wrong for doing such a great work to honor God? But that night in a dream God told Nathan to tell David not to build Him a house. Why did God not want David to build Him a house? God knew that David's motive for building Him a house was not because of his love for God, but to cover up his love for his own house of cedars. In a way, God was warning David not to let his love for his house and a life of ease to overcome David's desire to stay in the light of God by putting God first in his life.

We already saw in Chapter 10 that David stayed home when he should have gone to battle. The victories in chapter 10 only came when David left his house and went to fight the Syrians. Yet, he didn't finish the job against the Ammorites. That would come the next year, when David should have led the army, but instead he once again stayed behind. After all, nothing really bad happened when he stayed home the first time instead of going out with his army. So he continued to drift from God.

Another way David tried to cover up his feelings of guilt for loving his house more than he should was inviting Mephibosheth into his home. Yes, he had promised Jonathan that he would look after his family if anything happened to Jonathan, but some time had lapsed between the time David became King and the time he remembered that promise.

The first time he felt guilty about his love for his house, he tried to cover-up those feelings by appeasing God, but God knew the real motive and let it be known He was content to live in a tent, as David should have been. Since God wouldn't let him cover-up his sin by doing something apparently good, he sent for the son of Jonathan. Do you think that perhaps his motive for honoring Mephibosheth had more to do with covering his own sin than it did for his love of Jonathan? Sure, he loved Jonathan and he did good to remember his promise, but David knew he was wrong for the way he felt about his house, yet he would not be honest with himself, and God, by confessing what appears to be a minor sin. Yet that minor unconfessed sin led to so much more.

*2 And it came to pass in an eveningtide, that David arose from off his bed, and walked upon the roof of the king's house: and from the roof he saw a woman washing herself; and the woman was very beautiful to look upon.*

*3 And David sent and enquired after the woman. And one said, Is not this Bathsheba, the daughter of Eliam, the wife of Uriah the Hittite?*

*4 And David sent messengers, and took her; and she came in unto him, and he lay with her; for she was purified from her uncleanness: and she returned unto her house.*

Again, where was David while his army was laying siege to Rabbah? According to verse 2 he was lying in bed in his wonderful house of cedars. Being bored, he decided to enjoy the evening air and take a walk on his roof. That would be tantamount to sitting on the porch today. By the time he goes up on his roof, he has already slipped away from being in the center of the light of God.

When God spoke of the "house of David," he was referring to his family and lineage, but when David thought of his house he thought of his palace of cedars. When God said in II Sam. 7:16 that He would establish his house forever, He was referring to the coming Messiah who would come from the lineage of David. He had already warned David in the two verses previous that, *"If he commit iniquity, I will chasten him with the rod of men, and with the stripes of the children of men."*

So now David stands on his roof and looks down on Bathsheba and desires her. After all, why shouldn't he have her? He was the King, and as he told his wife Michal in II Sam. 6:22, *"..., and of the maidservants which thou hast spoken of, of them shall I be had in honor."* In other words, he knew he was desirable to other women and his own pride had allowed him to think more highly of himself than he should have. In the eyes of the world David had a lot to be proud of, but in truth, David was where he was because God had given him all the tools and favors he needed to be a great King.

*5 And the woman conceived, and sent and told David, and said, I am with child.*

*6 And David sent to Joab, saying, Send me Uriah the Hittite. And Joab sent Uriah to David.*

*7 And when Uriah was come unto him, David demanded of him how Joab did, and how the people did, and how the war prospered.*

*8 And David said to Uriah, Go down to thy house, and wash thy feet. And Uriah departed out of the king's house, and there followed him a mess of meat from the king.*

*9 But Uriah slept at the door of the king's house with all the servants of his lord, and went not down to his house.*

*10 And when they had told David, saying, Uriah went not down unto his house, David said unto Uriah, Camest thou not from thy journey? why then didst thou not go down unto thine house?*

*11 And Uriah said unto David, The ark, and Israel, and Judah, abide in tents; and my lord Joab, and the servants of my lord, are encamped in the open fields; shall I then go into mine house, to eat and to drink, and to lie with my wife? as thou livest, and as thy soul liveth, I will not do this thing.*

*12 And David said to Uriah, Tarry here to day also, and to morrow I will let thee depart. So Uriah abode in Jerusalem that day, and the morrow.*

*13 And when David had called him, he did eat and drink before him; and he made him drunk: and at even he went out to lie on his bed with the servants of his lord, but went not down to his house.*

*14 And it came to pass in the morning, that David wrote a letter to Joab, and sent it by the hand of Uriah.*

*15 And he wrote in the letter, saying, Set ye Uriah in the forefront of the hottest battle, and retire ye from him, that he may be smitten, and die.*

So, David gave in to his own desires and committed adultery with the wife of one of his mighty men of valor, Uriah the Hittite (II Sam. 23:39). We can choose our sins, but we cannot choose the consequences of our sin. In verse 5 of chapter 11 he hears the news he didn't want to hear when Bathsheba told David, *"I am with child."*

Now David can see he has a problem because it will be manifest in human flesh and then there will be a lot of explaining to do. At this point he has a choice, does he confess his sins and fall on the mercy of God, or does he try to cover it up? What would we do? What do we do? Too often we do just as David did. David considers his options and decides the best course of action to take is to recall her husband from the army so he can deny the baby is his if it ever comes up.

Would anybody else really know, though? Let's take a look at that possibility. In verse 4 he sent messengers to bring her to him after asking about her in verse 3. In verse 3 he found out who her father was and who her husband was. Her father was the son of Ahithophel, David's counselor (II Sam. 15:12 and II Sam. 23:34. Note that Eliam the son of Ahithophel, was the father of Bathsheba according to II Sam. 11:3. Therefore, David committed adultery with, and killed the husband of the granddaughter of his counselor.) I'm sure everyone in the palace knew of Bathsheba, because David had used his messengers and servants to find out just who she was and to deliver her unto him. He knew she was the granddaughter of his counselor, yet he still went through with it. To so blatantly commit a sin is a profound act of arrogance, a result of pride, which God hates. Our own sins are acts of arrogance against God.

So David calls for Uriah, the husband of Bathsheba, so he can blame her pregnancy on the husband and deflect any blame from himself should it ever come up. However, Uriah was not going to cooperate because he slept at the door of the David's house, instead of going to his own. David wouldn't leave his house, now Uriah wouldn't enter his. By this time, I think it's safe to say, the servants were on to David's plan concerning Uriah, so they reported to him that Uriah didn't go to his house. Now what is David to do? He calls Uriah and wants to know why he didn't go home. Of course, he couches this all in his own concern and love for one of his mighty men, but imagine the servants looks to each other, because they know the real motive to David's question.

Uriah's answer to the question should have cut David and allowed him to see his sin, and the very beginning source of that sin. In verse 11 Uriah tells David that God and Israel, and Joab and everyone else is encamped in the open fields, so how could he enjoy the pleasures of his home when no one else could? However, it would be painfully obvious that the only other one who was not where he was supposed to be was King David.

Was Uriah speaking to David what the rest of Israel was thinking? "Why was King David home while everyone else was off doing their duty?" Maybe David missed the implication; after all, he was too busy trying to cover up his sin than being open to a subtle reprimand. When we stick our heads in the sand in order to avoid confronting our sin, it keeps us from missing so many other things at the same time. We like to think our denial of sin is selective, that we can compartmentalize our wrong behavior, but blindness is not selective.

Therefore, in another effort to get Uriah to go to his wife, David gets him drunk. Once again, David is foiled when Uriah refuses to go to be with his wife. David now sees his only option is to make Bathsheba a widow so he can become her husband and have a child by her, all the while hoping no one would make the connection between the date of the marriage and date of the birth of the child. Uriah must die.

Notice which option David never even considered, and the option that today would be the first choice of most in the same predicament. Why didn't David just order an abortion? It is one thing to have an innocent man killed in battle, but an entirely different thing to have a pure innocent baby killed in the womb. Murder he could commit; abortion he could not.

*16 And it came to pass, when Joab observed the city, that he assigned Uriah unto a place where he knew that valiant men were.*

## The Edge of Darkness

*17 And the men of the city went out, and fought with Joab: and there fell some of the people of the servants of David; and Uriah the Hittite died also.*

*18 Then Joab sent and told David all the things concerning the war;*

*19 And charged the messenger, saying, When thou hast made an end of telling the matters of the war unto the king,*

*20 And if so be that the king's wrath arise, and he say unto thee, Wherefore approached ye so nigh unto the city when ye did fight? knew ye not that they would shoot from the wall?*

*21 Who smote Abimelech the son of Jerubbesheth? did not a woman cast a piece of a millstone upon him from the wall, that he died in Thebez? why went ye nigh the wall? then say thou, Thy servant Uriah the Hittite is dead also.*

*22 So the messenger went, and came and shewed David all that Joab had sent him for.*

*23 And the messenger said unto David, Surely the men prevailed against us, and came out unto us into the field, and we were upon them even unto the entering of the gate.*

*24 And the shooters shot from off the wall upon thy servants; and some of the king's servants be dead, and thy servant Uriah the Hittite is dead also.*

*25 Then David said unto the messenger, Thus shalt thou say unto Joab, Let not this thing displease thee, for the sword devoureth one as well as another: make thy battle more strong against the city, and overthrow it: and encourage thou him.*

*26 And when the wife of Uriah heard that Uriah her husband was dead, she mourned for her husband.*

*27 And when the mourning was past, David sent and fetched her to his house, and she became his wife, and bare him a son. But the thing that David had done displeased the LORD.*

David had involved his messengers and his servants in his sin, and now he is going to involve his general and his soldiers fighting at the front. David tells Joab to put Uriah in the thick of battle and then to abandon him so that he is sure to be killed. However, things aren't that simple. Uriah was one of 37 men of valor (II Sam. 23:37). That would make Uriah a commander of men who had their respect and devotion. How do you tell his men to follow him into battle and then to abandon their leader? The simple answer is you don't. To kill Uriah, many of his men are also going to have to die needlessly. Many more wives and children are going to be affected than just Bathsheba. And Joab, his general, is going to know he has ordered men into a death trap because he was directed to do so by his king.

In verse 16 Joab observed the most dangerous place, within shot of the walls of the city, and ordered Uriah and his men to attack knowing full well they would be killed. Verses 20 and 21 show that that strategy was flawed, and everyone, including Uriah and his men, plus the rest of the army observing, knew it was a flawed strategy. Do you think this caused many to lose confidence in David? The obvious answer is yes.

How did David react to the news of this defeat? If Joab hadn't been following his orders, David would have been angry with his general and most likely have reprimanded him in some way. Imagine the messengers, servants, counselors and the rest of his court standing around as the news of the battle is conveyed to David. I can imagine their concern with the news of the battle, but when they hear those final words at the end of the report, "Thy servant Uriah the Hittite is dead also." Then I suspect knowing glances were made across the room as the motive of the king became clear and they all realized that the battle was lost and men died to cover up the king's messing around with another man's wife.

Most likely the only two people that hadn't heard the talk about the king's illicit behavior were King David and Bathsheba. As far as Bathsheba knew, her husband had always been at the front and had died a hero's death. She did as she should have done and she mourned her lost husband. Was there any relief for her knowing she at least wouldn't have to face his questions about whose baby she was

## The Edge of Darkness

going to have, seeing as he had been away when she became pregnant? Was she guilty of adultery too? No, I do not believe she was guilty of adultery because she had had no choice. What David had done was tantamount to rape. It is clear that God held David responsible and not Bathsheba. Bathsheba would have to have answered to Uriah, but David had to answer to God. That is how God established the family – wives responsible to husbands and husbands responsible to God.

At the end of the chapter, once the mourning period was over, David brought Bathsheba into his house and made her his wife. David thought he got away with murder, though I'm sure David didn't think of his actions as murder since I'm sure he rationalized his sin just as we rationalize ours. The very last words of the chapter read, *"But the thing that David had done displeased the Lord."*

We often think that when God gets mad at us and our sin that he then punishes us by sending bad things into our life. He really doesn't have to do that. You see, there are natural consequences to sin. God was displeased not because his feelings were hurt that David loved his house more than Him. He was displeased because now David, whom he loved, was going to suffer along with so many others. He was displeased because now those who knew God through the life of David would now be in danger of having their faith in the God of David shaken.

David's love for his house and the ease of his life blinded him willingly to the dangers before him. In his position as king, his sin had far reaching affects, more and further than David ever believed possible. Our own sin has the same effect on our life and the lives of those connected with us. Maybe our influence isn't as far reaching as a king, but it reaches at least as far as our family and to those we love most.

# Chapter 12

## Repentance

*II Samuel Chapter XII*

*1 And the LORD sent Nathan unto David. And he came unto him, and said unto him, There were two men in one city; the one rich, and the other poor.*

*2 The rich man had exceeding many flocks and herds:*

*3 But the poor man had nothing, save one little ewe lamb, which he had bought and nourished up: and it grew up together with him, and with his children; it did eat of his own meat, and drank of his own cup, and lay in his bosom, and was unto him as a daughter.*

*4 And there came a traveller unto the rich man, and he spared to take of his own flock and of his own herd, to dress for the wayfaring man that was come unto him; but took the poor man's lamb, and dressed it for the man that was come to him.*

*5 And David's anger was greatly kindled against the man; and he said to Nathan, As the LORD liveth, the man that hath done this thing shall surely die:*

*6 And he shall restore the lamb fourfold, because he did this thing, and because he had no pity.*

Nathan, a prophet of God who served God by giving David confirmations and nudges when he needed it, did not go to David on his own accord, but went when prompted to do so by God. Notice he doesn't confront David with his sin head on, but rather he uses an analogy to convict David of his sin. David, having drifted from the center of the light of God, and having hid his head in the sand so long, doesn't find anything about the analogy familiar.

Allow me to momentarily offer another picture of this analogy that you may not have seen before. The analogy presents us a rich man, a poor man, a traveler and a lamb. When Jesus Christ came to earth, he was a precious lamb to many of the poor people who followed him as he sought to establish his Kingdom. However, the rich men being the priests and leaders of Israel, were afraid of losing their place at the top, so they took the lamb from the poor people, or in this case, the lamb went peacefully to the slaughter so that the traveler could be served to nourish his life. The traveler could be us, the church. Christ gave himself for the church, where we were once strangers, now we are sons.

David's reaction to this callous disregard for the property of another that was so unjust was to pronounce the accused guilty and then to sentence the accused to death. The problem was, David did not realize that he was the accused and he was passing judgment on himself. David knew all along he was wrong and he was sinning, but through his own justification of his actions and willfulness to hide his head in the sand, he would not allow himself to see the truth.

*7 And Nathan said to David, Thou art the man. Thus saith the LORD God of Israel, I anointed thee king over Israel, and I delivered thee out of the hand of Saul;*

*8 And I gave thee thy master's house, and thy master's wives into thy bosom, and gave thee the house of Israel and of Judah; and if that had been too little, I would moreover have given unto thee such and such things.*

*9 Wherefore hast thou despised the commandment of the LORD, to do evil in his sight? thou hast killed Uriah the Hittite with the sword, and hast taken his wife to be thy wife, and hast slain him with the sword of the children of Ammon.*

*10 Now therefore the sword shall never depart from thine house; because thou hast despised me, and hast taken the wife of Uriah the Hittite to be thy wife.*

*11 Thus saith the LORD, Behold, I will raise up evil against thee out of thine own house, and I will take thy wives before thine eyes, and give them unto thy neighbour, and he shall lie with thy wives in the sight of this sun.*

*12 For thou didst it secretly: but I will do this thing before all Israel, and before the sun.*

However, God has a way of exposing the truth to us so that we are forced to confront our own sin. Not only had David pronounced the death sentence, but he also ordered the accused to restore to the poor man four-fold. In this case the sentence could not be carried out as David ordered because of extenuating circumstances. The poor man, being Uriah, had been killed as a result of the orders of David to make sure he would die in battle. So, restitution could not be paid. The death penalty had been ordered, but could David order his own execution? Interestingly, in verse 13 Nathan told David that God had put away his sin and that he wouldn't die. The just thing would have been for David to die for his sin, but God is merciful and vacated the death sentence against David. Thankfully, God is merciful, because we also had a death sentence on us, which God vacates as soon as we put our trust in Jesus Christ so that God can then forgive our sins.

So, David's anger is kindled as he pronounces judgment, but then Nathan cuts to the heart of David by uttering these simple words, *"Thou art the man."* David, in his arrogance, had thought he had gotten away with murder. But God knows all and if chooses, he can reveal all. David's sin was going to affect the entire nation, so now the entire nation was going to know the source of their troubles, which was the sin of David. Israel had been blessed because of the conduct of David, and now they would suffer because of the conduct of David.

In verses 7 and 8 God reminds David of what he had forgotten. He was the source of David's position, wealth and house. We sometimes may be tempted to think more highly of ourselves than we should, as David had done, but we must remember that God gives us all, and that any talent we may have was given to us by God.

In verse 9 it is written, "Wherefore hast thou despised the commandment of the Lord, to do evil in his sight?" How many of the 10 commandments had David broken? By my count he broke at least 6 directly. Notice, however, that when God rebuked him He spoke in the singular. The one commandment on which all others hinge is the first, "Thou shalt have no other gods before me." (Ex. 20:3)

David had allowed his own pride in his house and his accomplishments to crowd out God in his life. God first reminded David those accomplishments and that house was David's because God had given them to him. Now in verses 10-12 God pronounces the results of David's sin. The house that David had loved so much would be filled with violence and the sword would not depart from it. The evil God will raise up against David will come from within his own house and his wives will be taken by other men in plain sight. Whereas David had committed his sin in secret, God would bring out everything and the deeds done against David will be done in the open.

*13 And David said unto Nathan, I have sinned against the LORD. And Nathan said unto David, The LORD also hath put away thy sin; thou shalt not die.*

*14 Howbeit, because by this deed thou hast given great occasion to the enemies of the LORD to blaspheme, the child also that is born unto thee shall surely die.*

*15 And Nathan departed unto his house. And the LORD struck the child that Uriah's wife bare unto David, and it was very sick.*

*16 David therefore besought God for the child; and David fasted, and went in, and lay all night upon the earth.*

*17 And the elders of his house arose, and went to him, to raise him up from the earth: but he would not, neither did he eat bread with them.*

*18 And it came to pass on the seventh day, that the child died. And the servants of David feared to tell him that the child was dead: for they said, Behold, while the child was yet alive, we spake unto him, and he would not hearken unto our voice: how will he then vex himself, if we tell him that the child is dead?*

*19 But when David saw that his servants whispered, David perceived that the child was dead: therefore David said unto his servants, Is the child dead? And they said, He is dead.*

In verse 13 David finally confesses his sin and his heart breaks. When Saul admitted his sin to God, it seems his heart never broke as a result of that sin. Here, when David admits his guilt before the Lord, God has accepted that confession and forgiven him.

## A Man After God's Own Heart

**When God said David was a man after his own heart, perhaps this is one of the things that made it so. God's heart grieves over sin, and so did David's. Sin, especially our own sin, should grieve us as it does God.**

Saul never did seem to get his heart to grieve. Let us be sure to have a heart open to the love of God, for that is where the ability to love comes from. And when one loves, one hurts when that fellowship is broken with the one you love. David's sin had broken fellowship with the one he loved – God, and now that heart was broken.

In verse 14 God let's David know the child to be born of Bathsheba will die. On the surface it may seem as if God is using the death of the child to punish David, but that is not the motive behind the death of the child. God was showing mercy to the child by going ahead and taking it home to heaven instead of leaving it here to suffer the ridicule that would have come for being the bastard child of the king. Taking the baby was God's decision, and not David's.

Next in verses 15-18 David fasts and prays over the child in the hope that God would change His mind and spare the life of the baby. He seemed so distraught to his servants that they worried what he would do if the baby did die. Also, remember that one of his counselors that would have been present was the grandfather of Bathsheba, meaning that it was his great-grandson that would die as a result of David's sin. We will see later what problems this is going to cause.

Finally, in verse 19 the baby dies and his servants are afraid to tell him; however, now that David is not burying his head in the sand, he is able to see the truth of what is going on around him, and he perceives that the baby is dead.

*20 Then David arose from the earth, and washed, and anointed himself, and changed his apparel, and came into the house of the LORD, and worshipped: then he came to his own house; and when he required, they set bread before him, and he did eat.*

*21 Then said his servants unto him, What thing is this that thou hast done? thou didst fast and weep for the child, while it was alive; but when the child was dead, thou didst rise and eat bread.*

*22 And he said, While the child was yet alive, I fasted and wept: for I said, Who can tell whether GOD will be gracious to me, that the child may live?*

*23 But now he is dead, wherefore should I fast? can I bring him back again? I shall go to him, but he shall not return to me.*

*24 And David comforted Bathsheba his wife, and went in unto her, and lay with her: and she bare a son, and he called his name Solomon: and the LORD loved him.*

*25 And he sent by the hand of Nathan the prophet; and he called his name Jedidiah, because of the LORD.*

Notice where David goes once he prepared himself through washing and anointing himself. He first goes to the house of the Lord and then his own house. Had David's priorities changed? He had wandered from the Lord because he had fallen more in love with his house than with God, so now that he had been forced to confront his own sin and repented with a broken heart, God was now first in his life again.

Instead of going into a period of mourning, as his servants expected him to do, David instead does the exact opposite, to the confusion

## Repentance

of those around him. David states his reasons for not mourning in the traditional way. He cannot bring the baby back, but his next words should be comforting to all who have lost a loved one, especially if the loss was that of a child. David said he would go to him. The baby went to paradise and upon David's death he will join his child there.

The father had lost his son, but the mother had lost her son also, and David, who is now sensitive to others again, goes to the woman who is now his wife, Bathsheba, and comforts her. They once again have a son and his name is Solomon. The children of David before Bathsheba saw their father fall and commit grievous sins against the family and against God. Solomon would not know that father. The father he knew was a repentant and broken man. He was now a good man who had suffered as a result of his sin and would raise, in Solomon, a man worthy of the throne. Not only did David love Solomon; the Lord also loved Solomon.

Circumstances and the results of sin can change us. How many of us are the same person we were in high school? When someone falls, as David did, how long do we continue to shun and punish them? Are we willing to forgive once the guilty has repented? The results of sin do not have to be a life sentence. Let us be willing to forgive others as we wish them to forgive us and our transgressions.

*26 And Joab fought against Rabbah of the children of Ammon, and took the royal city.*

*27 And Joab sent messengers to David, and said, I have fought against Rabbah, and have taken the city of waters.*

*28 Now therefore gather the rest of the people together, and encamp against the city, and take it: lest I take the city, and it be called after my name.*

*29 And David gathered all the people together, and went to Rabbah, and fought against it, and took it.*

*30 And he took their king's crown from off his head, the weight whereof was a talent of gold with the precious stones: and it was set on David's head. And he brought forth the spoil of the city in great abundance.*

*31 And he brought forth the people that were therein, and put them under saws, and under harrows of iron, and under axes of iron, and made them pass through the brickkiln: and thus did he unto all the cities of the children of Ammon. So David and all the people returned unto Jerusalem.*

In verses 26-31 we leave the story of David and Bathsheba and the consequences of their sin and return to the circumstances at hand. While David was fasting and praying for the life of his child with Bathsheba, Joab is winning the victory over Rabbah. David may have been willing to try to steal God's glory, but Joab knew better than try to steal the glory of the king, and so he sent messengers to David and told him to come so that he may claim the victory.

The Ammonites had been defeated and David entered the city as the conquering hero. On the surface it doesn't appear that David is going to suffer for his sin. Keep in mind that it takes some time to grow a crop, and that includes a crop of wild oats. We often plant corrupted crops and then pray for crop failure. On the surface it may have seemed nothing had changed, but David knew better. Waiting can be a very hard thing to do.

When my son was young and would need to be punished, I would send him to his room and tell him I would be up in a little while to administer punishment. Then I would wait. It gave him time to think about what he had done and the possible consequences, and then time to regret his actions that had him awaiting his punishment. By the time I made it to his room to administer punishment, it was easier to show mercy because not only was I calmer, but my son had already been suffering for his actions.

# Chapter 13

## Example to Our Children

*II Samuel Chapter XIII*

*1 And it came to pass after this, that Absalom the son of David had a fair sister, whose name was Tamar; and Amnon the son of David loved her.*

*2 And Amnon was so vexed, that he fell sick for his sister Tamar; for she was a virgin; and Amnon thought it hard for him to do any thing to her.*

*3 But Amnon had a friend, whose name was Jonadab, the son of Shimeah David's brother: and Jonadab was a very subtil man.*

*4 And he said unto him, Why art thou, being the king's son, lean from day to day? wilt thou not tell me? And Amnon said unto him, I love Tamar, my brother Absalom's sister.*

*5 And Jonadab said unto him, Lay thee down on thy bed, and make thyself sick: and when thy father cometh to see thee, say unto him, I pray thee, let my sister Tamar come, and give me meat, and dress the meat in my sight, that I may see it, and eat it at her hand.*

*6 So Amnon lay down, and made himself sick: and when the king was come to see him, Amnon said unto the king, I pray thee, let Tamar my sister come, and make me a couple of cakes in my sight, that I may eat at her hand.*

*7 Then David sent home to Tamar, saying, Go now to thy brother Amnon's house, and dress him meat.*

> *8 So Tamar went to her brother Amnon's house; and he was laid down. And she took flour, and kneaded it, and made cakes in his sight, and did bake the cakes.*
>
> *9 And she took a pan, and poured them out before him; but he refused to eat. And Amnon said, Have out all men from me. And they went out every man from him.*
>
> *10 And Amnon said unto Tamar, Bring the meat into the chamber, that I may eat of thine hand. And Tamar took the cakes which she had made, and brought them into the chamber to Amnon her brother.*
>
> *11 And when she had brought them unto him to eat, he took hold of her, and said unto her, Come lie with me, my sister.*

Now we begin to see the consequences of David's sin played out.

Absalom and Tamar were brother and sister, with David and Maacha being their parents (II Sam. 3:3). David had another son by a different mother – Amnon who was obsessed with Tamar. However, Amnon was afraid of his older half-brother Absalom, it would seem, because he wouldn't approach her.

We are not told how old Amnon is, but it would appear he's still not quite confident in his manhood. He doesn't quite know what to do about this infatuation he has with his half-sister, which he thinks is love. Things are so bad that he's not eating right and so his cousin Jonadab asks him what's wrong (vs 4).

The Bible describes Jonadab as a subtle man (vs 3) and in his question to Amnon he seems to say, "What do you have to worry about, you're the king's son." We sometimes think that just because a person comes from a prosperous or well-known family that they have it made. However, wealth and fame do not bring happiness. In this case, Amnon wanted something he didn't think he could have, and that was his half-sister, Tamar. So Jonadab hatches a plan for Amnon that will give him the opportunity to let her know how he feels. Things are going to go terribly wrong, though.

## Example to Our Children

Jonadab's plan was for Amnon to fake a sickness so he could have his sister sent to him so she could take care of him. Jonadab was telling Amnon to manipulate his father and sister so he could get what he wanted.

What should Amnon have done? He should have sought God. He did not look to God, however. He could also have sought the council of a Godly man, perhaps Nathan, but he did not do that either. He could have gone to his father, King David, to ask advice, but he chose not to. He had witnessed his father's transgression, so maybe by manipulating the situation like his father; he could get what he wanted.

Is it easier to do right or do wrong? Sin comes naturally, whereas we must work to do right. We often look for ways to justify our behavior, so one of the things we do is look to where our parents, or someone else we look up to, have failed and repeat the same mistake, as if somehow when we do it we'll get away with it.

Tamar comes and makes Amnon cakes so that he could watch her and admire her as she worked. Amnon thought he was in love with her, but in reality he was in lust for her. He must have been fantasizing for a very long time how good it would be to spend some intimate time with her; so much so that it became his goal above all else. In verse 11 he takes her by the hand and says, "Come lie with me, my sister."

*12 And she answered him, Nay, my brother, do not force me; for no such thing ought to be done in Israel: do not thou this folly.*

*13 And I, whither shall I cause my shame to go? and as for thee, thou shalt be as one of the fools in Israel. Now therefore, I pray thee, speak unto the king; for he will not withhold me from thee.*

*14 Howbeit he would not hearken unto her voice: but, being stronger than she, forced her, and lay with her.*

*15 Then Amnon hated her exceedingly; so that the hatred wherewith he hated her was greater than the love wherewith he had loved her. And Amnon said unto her, Arise, be gone.*

*16 And she said unto him, There is no cause: this evil in sending me away is greater than the other that thou didst unto me. But he would not hearken unto her.*

*17 Then he called his servant that ministered unto him, and said, Put now this woman out from me, and bolt the door after her.*

*18 And she had a garment of divers colours upon her: for with such robes were the king's daughters that were virgins apparelled. Then his servant brought her out, and bolted the door after her.*

*19 And Tamar put ashes on her head, and rent her garment of divers colours that was on her, and laid her hand on her head, and went on crying.*

Her response was to resist and remind him to do such a thing was a folly. Did he listen? He wasn't thinking rationally, he was thinking with his passions and it was that, that doomed him and that is what dooms us. She even tries to explain how bad this will be for her in verse 13 when she says in essence, *"I will have to live with this shame the rest of my life."* If Amnon had truly loved her he would have wanted the best for her, and to subject her to the shame of what he was about to do is not an act of love, it's an act of power and betrayal.

She goes on in the same verse and tells him to talk to their father, King David, so that he could give her to Amnon in a proper way. She appeared to be willing to marry Amnon, or she was in the least trying to convince him, however she could, not to rape her. He did not listen to her sound reasoning and proceeded to rape her.

Amnon must have thought that by having his way with her finally after all this time, he would somehow be satisfied and that passion in him was pure love. But love doesn't force, and that passion converted itself into hate. He should have hated himself, and maybe he did, but he took out his hate on Tamar and ordered her from his presence.

She pleaded with him not to do this second shame to her in verse 16, but Amnon cared nothing for Tamar, he only cared about himself. By raping her he had defiled her and ruined her for any other man. She had worn a special coat that designated her as a virgin, but now she ripped the coat and mourned her lost virginity and was distraught at the evil that had been perpetuated against her.

*20 And Absalom her brother said unto her, Hath Amnon thy brother been with thee? but hold now thy peace, my sister: he is thy brother; regard not this thing. So Tamar remained desolate in her brother Absalom's house.*

*21 But when king David heard of all these things, he was very wroth.*

*22 And Absalom spake unto his brother Amnon neither good nor bad: for Absalom hated Amnon, because he had forced his sister Tamar.*

*23 And it came to pass after two full years, that Absalom had sheepshearers in Baalhazor, which is beside Ephraim: and Absalom invited all the king's sons.*

*24 And Absalom came to the king, and said, Behold now, thy servant hath sheepshearers; let the king, I beseech thee, and his servants go with thy servant.*

*25 And the king said to Absalom, Nay, my son, let us not all now go, lest we be chargeable unto thee. And he pressed him: howbeit he would not go, but blessed him.*

*26 Then said Absalom, If not, I pray thee, let my brother Amnon go with us. And the king said unto him, Why should he go with thee?*

*27 But Absalom pressed him, that he let Amnon and all the king's sons go with him.*

*28 Now Absalom had commanded his servants, saying, Mark ye now when Amnon's heart is merry with wine, and when I say unto you, Smite Amnon; then kill him, fear not: have not I commanded you? be courageous, and be valiant.*

*29 And the servants of Absalom did unto Amnon as Absalom had commanded. Then all the king's sons arose, and every man gat him up upon his mule, and fled.*

*30 And it came to pass, while they were in the way, that tidings came to David, saying, Absalom hath slain all the king's sons, and there is not one of them left.*

*31 Then the king arose, and tare his garments, and lay on the earth; and all his servants stood by with their clothes rent.*

*32 And Jonadab, the son of Shimeah David's brother, answered and said, Let not my lord suppose that they have slain all the young men the king's sons; for Amnon only is dead: for by the appointment of Absalom this hath been determined from the day that he forced his sister Tamar.*

*33 Now therefore let not my lord the king take the thing to his heart, to think that all the king's sons are dead: for Amnon only is dead.*

*34 But Absalom fled. And the young man that kept the watch lifted up his eyes, and looked, and, behold, there came much people by the way of the hill side behind him.*

*35 And Jonadab said unto the king, Behold, the king's sons come: as thy servant said, so it is.*

*36 And it came to pass, as soon as he had made an end of speaking, that, behold, the king's sons came, and lifted up their voice and wept: and the king also and all his servants wept very sore.*

*37 But Absalom fled, and went to Talmai, the son of Ammihud, king of Geshur. And David mourned for his son every day.*

*38 So Absalom fled, and went to Geshur, and was there three years.*

*39 And the soul of king David longed to go forth unto Absalom: for he was comforted concerning Amnon, seeing he was dead.*

In verse 20 Absalom, the brother that loved her so much, who had named his daughter after her (II Sam. 14:27), saw how distraught she was and immediately guessed who had hurt her so badly. He asked, "Hath Amnon thy brother been with thee?" When we genuinely love someone as Absalom loved his sister, then we are more observant and sensitive to them than usual. He could sense Amnon was fascinated with Tamar, but he never expected his half-brother would do such an evil thing.

We might expect Absalom to go after Amnon in a fit of rage, but instead he was cold and calculating. He would bide his time until he gained his revenge. He told Tamar not to worry about it and he tried to put the best face on the situation as he could for her, but Absalom now hated his brother for how he had hurt someone he cared so much about.

So, he waits, he waits two whole years to exact his revenge. He also gives his father two years to meet out the justice that should have been carried out, but King David does nothing. When the law isn't just, people are apt to take justice into their own hands, and that's just what Absalom does.

After two years (vs 23) Absalom is ready to take his revenge. It was time to shear the sheep in Baal-hazor, and I imagine this may have been like barn raisings in America in olden times when neighbors got together to do the work and used the time as a time of fellowship. I remember when I was younger getting jobs in the hayfields. We worked very hard until dinner time, and then we all made our way to the farmhouse where the farmer's wife had prepared a great meal. Those were good times as we ate our meals and spent time with our friends.

Absalom first invited his father, King David, to the shearing, but he declined (vs 25). There are a few possibilities here as to why Absalom invited David. Maybe he was wanting some son-father time, or maybe he was trying to throw off David's suspicion when he invited Amnon. When he did suggest taking Amnon with him, David's suspicion does seem to be aroused because he asks why he would want to take Amnon (vs 26). Absalom must have countered by claiming to want to take all of his brothers. He kept on asking David and he finally gave in and made it possible for all of them to go, including Amnon.

Absalom's plan was to wait until Amnon got drunk, then have his servants kill his brother for what he did to Tamar. Just as David had the Ammorites kill Uriah, Abaslom has his servants kill Amnon, which they did in verse 29. This caused all the brothers to flee, for what they expected was their lives. Throughout history it was not uncommon for those in line to the throne to kill those who may be in competition with them.

In verse 30 that is exactly what was told to King David, that all his sons had been killed, and so he fell to the ground in mourning after renting his clothes, as did those around the king. Jonadab, the very one who had counseled Amnon to fake being sick so he could be with his sister Tamar, is the one who tells the king that it was only Amnon who had been killed, and not the rest of David's sons. He knew of Absalom's plan to kill Amnon, because he tells David that only Amnon had been killed. As the old saying goes, "With friends like that, who needs enemies?"

It doesn't seem that David picked up on Jonadab's previous knowledge of the planned execution of Amnon. In verse 35 Jonadab gloats and says in essence, "I told you so," when the lookout spotted the rest of the sons of David returning from Baal-hazor. All of his sons that is, except for Absalom who fled to Geshur, where his grandfather on his mother's side lived.

David mourned for Absalom, but he didn't do anything to make things right with his son. During this whole episode, from Amnon raping Tamar to Absalom executing Amnon, King David does nothing to see that anyone is brought to justice for their crime. He was aware that Amnon had raped his daughter and it seems it was a relief to him when he learned that justice had been served on Amnon. However, justice should have been served by the king, not the king's son and one of the victims of the crime.

Why did David once again stick his head in the sand when it came to meeting out justice to his own family? Perhaps the reason is he felt he had lost his moral authority. After all, why would his sons listen to him when he had done even worse? Is this a sufficient excuse to act as David was acting? No, we are all sinners and when David repented it is up to him to reestablish his moral authority. It takes time, but those around us should see our change and in time they may listen again. We have one thing we are responsible to do, and that is to do right. Confidence can never be restored if we continue to do wrong because we're afraid we won't be listened to when we need to correct someone we're in authority over. Are we too afraid to do right because we're afraid of being ridiculed or scoffed at? Ask God to forgive you, forgive yourself, then do the right thing from then on out to the best of your ability with God's help.

# Chapter 14

## To Restore a Son

We use analogies to get our point across in a round-about way. By comparing two things, it often makes us understand the more difficult concept much easier. Jesus often used parables to convey a spiritual truth through a common story. Methods like this are used to open the minds of people and simplify a concept so it is more easily understood. In Chapter 12 Nathan used a story of a rich man taking a poor man's pet lamb to feed a stranger to convict David of his sin.

For whatever reason it seems to have helped to approach David through a story, or in this case, through a dramatic story being played out by an actress. In verse 1 Joab knew that David was missing his son Absalom and that his heart yearned for him. Yet David, for whatever reason, wouldn't even try to make peace.

David, as the king, could serve as a counselor and judge for the nation of Israel, but he would not council or judge his own family. So in verse 2 we see Joab put together a plan meant to reunite King David with his estranged son, Absalom. He hires a woman to tell a story to David that is similar to David's situation with Absalom, but different enough so that David might not notice the method being used in an attempt to reconcile father and son.

*II Samuel Chapter XIV*

*1 Now Joab the son of Zeruiah perceived that the king's heart was toward Absalom.*

*2 And Joab sent to Tekoah, and fetched thence a wise woman, and said unto her, I pray thee, feign thyself to be a mourner, and put on now mourning apparel, and anoint not thyself with oil, but be as a woman that had a long time mourned for the dead:*

*3 And come to the king, and speak on this manner unto him. So Joab put the words in her mouth.*

*4 And when the woman of Tekoah spake to the king, she fell on her face to the ground, and did obeisance, and said, Help, O king.*

*5 And the king said unto her, What aileth thee? And she answered, I am indeed a widow woman, and mine husband is dead.*

*6 And thy handmaid had two sons, and they two strove together in the field, and there was none to part them, but the one smote the other, and slew him.*

*7 And, behold, the whole family is risen against thine handmaid, and they said, Deliver him that smote his brother, that we may kill him, for the life of his brother whom he slew; and we will destroy the heir also: and so they shall quench my coal which is left, and shall not leave to my husband neither name nor remainder upon the earth.*

*8 And the king said unto the woman, Go to thine house, and I will give charge concerning thee.*

*9 And the woman of Tekoah said unto the king, My lord, O king, the iniquity be on me, and on my father's house: and the king and his throne be guiltless.*

*10 And the king said, Whosoever saith ought unto thee, bring him to me, and he shall not touch thee any more.*

*11 Then said she, I pray thee, let the king remember the LORD thy God, that thou wouldest not suffer the revengers of blood to destroy any more, lest they destroy my son. And he said, As the LORD liveth, there shall not one hair of thy son fall to the earth.*

*12 Then the woman said, Let thine handmaid, I pray thee, speak one word unto my lord the king. And he said, Say on.*

*13 And the woman said, Wherefore then hast thou thought such a thing against the people of God? for the king doth speak this thing as one which is faulty, in that the king doth not fetch home again his banished.*

*14 For we must needs die, and are as water spilt on the ground, which cannot be gathered up again; neither doth God respect any person: yet doth he devise means, that his banished be not expelled from him.*

In verses 3 through 12 the woman tells her story and David wastes no time in making his judgment of the matter. His judgment was that the woman's son was to go unharmed and that if anyone interfered she was to bring him before the king who would make sure they never bothered her again.

In verse 13 the woman makes clear that once again, David is the man. To paraphrase she says, "You seem to think the people of Israel will harm Absalom if you allow him to return to you."

Verse 14 is about David and Absalom, but it could just as easily be about God and you. Before salvation we are estranged from God and banished from his presence because of our guilt, but God has made a way of salvation so that the banished don't have to be banished forever. After our salvation, when we sin, we lose fellowship with God and sometimes we fear confessing that sin because of our guilt. Especially if it's a sin we keep committing over and over.

*15 Now therefore that I am come to speak of this thing unto my lord the king, it is because the people have made me afraid: and thy handmaid said, I will now speak unto the king; it may be that the king will perform the request of his handmaid.*

*16 For the king will hear, to deliver his handmaid out of the hand of the man that would destroy me and my son together out of the inheritance of God.*

*17 Then thine handmaid said, The word of my lord the king shall now be comfortable: for as an angel of God, so is my lord the king to discern good and bad: therefore the LORD thy God will be with thee.*

*18 Then the king answered and said unto the woman, Hide not from me, I pray thee, the thing that I shall ask thee. And the woman said, Let my lord the king now speak.*

*19 And the king said, Is not the hand of Joab with thee in all this? And the woman answered and said, As thy soul liveth, my lord the king, none can turn to the right hand or to the left from ought that my lord the king hath spoken: for thy servant Joab, he bade me, and he put all these words in the mouth of thine handmaid:*

*20 To fetch about this form of speech hath thy servant Joab done this thing: and my lord is wise, according to the wisdom of an angel of God, to know all things that are in the earth.*

*21 And the king said unto Joab, Behold now, I have done this thing: go therefore, bring the young man Absalom again.*

*22 And Joab fell to the ground on his face, and bowed himself, and thanked the king: and Joab said, To day thy servant knoweth that I have found grace in thy sight, my lord, O king, in that the king hath fulfilled the request of his servant.*

*23 So Joab arose and went to Geshur, and brought Absalom to Jerusalem.*

*24 And the king said, Let him turn to his own house, and let him not see my face. So Absalom returned to his own house, and saw not the king's face.*

Finally, in verse 19, David figures out that Joab has put her up to this and they are talking not about her son, but about David's son Absalom. So, David tells Joab to go and get Absalom and return him to Jerusalem. Yet in verse 24 he takes the wind right out of Joab's sails when he tells him to let Absalom return to his own house, but that he was not to see his father.

Ever since David's great sin he has tried avoiding any kind of confrontation within his family. Perhaps he thought he had lost his moral authority, or maybe he was being so careful not to give an opportunity for one of his son's to challenge his authority through violence, as God had said would happen through the prophet Nathan (II Sam. 12:10). However, try as we might, we cannot escape the judgment of God.

Joab's reaction is to simply be thankful for what he could get. I imagine he was disappointed that David still refused to see Absalom, but it was good to at least get some kind of concession.

*25 But in all Israel there was none to be so much praised as Absalom for his beauty: from the sole of his foot even to the crown of his head there was no blemish in him.*

*26 And when he polled his head, (for it was at every year's end that he polled it: because the hair was heavy on him, therefore he polled it:) he weighed the hair of his head at two hundred shekels after the king's weight.*

*27 And unto Absalom there were born three sons, and one daughter, whose name was Tamar: she was a woman of a fair countenance.*

*28 So Absalom dwelt two full years in Jerusalem, and saw not the king's face.*

*29 Therefore Absalom sent for Joab, to have sent him to the king; but he would not come to him: and when he sent again the second time, he would not come.*

*30 Therefore he said unto his servants, See, Joab's field is near mine, and he hath barley there; go and set it on fire. And Absalom's servants set the field on fire.*

*31 Then Joab arose, and came to Absalom unto his house, and said unto him, Wherefore have thy servants set my field on fire?*

*32 And Absalom answered Joab, Behold, I sent unto thee, saying, Come hither, that I may send thee to the king, to say, Wherefore am I come from Geshur? it had been good for me to have been there still: now therefore let me see the king's face; and if there be any iniquity in me, let him kill me.*

*33 So Joab came to the king, and told him: and when he had called for Absalom, he came to the king, and bowed himself on his face to the ground before the king: and the king kissed Absalom.*

Verse 25 gives us a description of the appearance of Absalom. He was a man the Bible describes as beautiful without a blemish on him. His hair was long and thick, that I'm sure every woman in Israel was jealous of his hair. We already know the value the people of Israel put on appearances. After all, they picked Saul to be their King because he looked like what they thought a king should look like. Even Samuel fell for this idea of outward appearance when he was going to anoint the next King of Israel from among Jesse's sons. We sometimes think we here in America are overly fixated on outward appearance, but it was no less true in the time of King David. We should pick our leaders, and everyone else we get to pick in our lives, based on Godly character. Instead, we base our choices on looks or the quality of their voice.

An interesting side note is included in verse 27. It tells us Absalom had three sons and a daughter named Tamar. Usually the Bible gives us the name of the sons, but in this case it gives us the name of his daughter and tells us that she too had a good appearance. It seems that Absalom must have named his daughter after his defiled sister Tamar. Obviously, Absalom had a very close and strong relationship with his sister, so it is no wonder he reacted as he did toward Amnon when David did nothing to bring Amnon to justice.

For two years Absalom waited for his father, King David, to do the right thing and send for him to restore their fellowship. Yet David did nothing. Again, it appears he feared to face his son for whatever reason. So, Absalom sends for the Joab twice. However, Joab does not come as he was bidden.

In verse 30 we find out just what kind of personality Absalom has when he takes matters into his own hands. To be ignored twice by Joab must have angered Absalom greatly, because he had a unique way of getting Joab's attention. After all, he was the king's son, a prince, and when he asks to see his father's general, he thought he should be respected enough to have his wish granted.

It does seem a little odd that Joab did not respond to Absalom's request. It must be remembered, though, that Joab didn't go to bring

Absalom back to Jerusalem because of his love for Absalom, he did so out of his love for his king – David.

So Absalom does what any person would do who feels slighted. He sets Joab's barley field on fire. That got Joab's attention. I must confess, I find a bit of humor in what Absalom does, and I have to think those who heard of what Absalom did must have chuckled as a result also.

Joab wanted to know what was so important that Absalom wanted to see him bad enough to burn down his barley field. Absalom simply wanted to see his father. I sense a son who loved his father, but who was resentful of his inaction and apparent indifference toward his own family. In one last-ditch effort to restore fellowship with his father, he asks Joab to arrange a meeting with him, and if his father finds fault in him, he would be willing to die for that fault.

So Absalom gets what he wants when the king grants him an audience and Absalom goes to bow before his father, and King David kisses him. This sounds good, but there also seems to be something missing. Fellowship is more than acceptance; fellowship is talking and being intimate with our thoughts and feelings. Absalom wanted fellowship, but his father would only grant him an audience.

In verse 39 of chapter 13 we see that David wanted to go to Absalom in a way that was described as longing. Yet he wouldn't allow himself to give in to his feelings for his son. When, after several years, Absalom is the one that makes the reunion happen, it is an empty reunion. Why David shut himself off from his own feelings for Absalom I'm not sure. Perhaps it was the guilt of his sin that still gnawed at him. Whatever the reason, his failure to allow the restoration of fellowship with his son would drive a wedge between them that would result in Absalom's rebellion.

As parents, we fear our children rebelling against our authority. And in our desire to see it's not done; we sometimes do those very things that drive our kids to rebel. How do you keep your child from rebelling? You give him a Godly example and pray. However, no matter our example, sometimes kids will rebel anyway. Still, when they've wronged us, we can't continue to hold that grudge, especially when they come to us. Do more than grant an audience for your wayward child, do whatever you can to restore the fellowship they are truly longing for. God has an unconditional love for His children. Do you have an unconditional love for yours?

# Chapter 15

## A Family Divided

*II Samuel Chapter XV*

*1 And it came to pass after this, that Absalom prepared him chariots and horses, and fifty men to run before him.*

*2 And Absalom rose up early, and stood beside the way of the gate: and it was so, that when any man that had a controversy came to the king for judgment, then Absalom called unto him, and said, Of what city art thou? And he said, Thy servant is of one of the tribes of Israel.*

*3 And Absalom said unto him, See, thy matters are good and right; but there is no man deputed of the king to hear thee.*

*4 Absalom said moreover, Oh that I were made judge in the land, that every man which hath any suit or cause might come unto me, and I would do him justice!*

*5 And it was so, that when any man came nigh to him to do him obeisance, he put forth his hand, and took him, and kissed him.*

*6 And on this manner did Absalom to all Israel that came to the king for judgment: so Absalom stole the hearts of the men of Israel.*

Absalom had given his father a chance to do the right thing, and in Absalom's eyes, his father had failed. Therefore, Absalom's thoughts turned to how, if he would be given the chance, he would do things better. He would be a better king. He would do things right. In his eyes he was justified in his actions that were to come because, "The old man had lost touch."

David was an old man by now in the eyes of the younger generation. If, as in verse 7, Absalom is around 40 years of age, then David is at least in his 60's. To Absalom his father had been a miserable failure as a father, and this equated to the belief he was being a miserable king as well. Since he was a prince, then why not set things up so he would become the next king over any of his brothers. After all, he was the most qualified son in his eyes and in the eyes of many around him who adored him because of his physical appearance.

In today's terms we would say he starts to assemble an entourage; an entourage, coincidentally, which would evolve into an army. He positioned himself at the gate as people came into the city to have the king solve their disputes and began undermining the king's authority.

He took a personal interest in them by asking them where they were from. He would then tell them no one was there for the king who could help them, but if he were king he would make sure that he would hear them and give them justice. He then became a glad-handing politician and would kiss them as we envision politicians kissing babies.

Isn't that the way of the person seeking to undermine the boss. They shake our heads and say, "If I were the boss, I'd do things a lot different." There is usually truth in what they say and in the beginning we may be drawn in by their meddling, but beware associating yourself too close with the rebel. In time their actions become troublesome and what usually happens is the only thing affected by their constant complaining is your attitude toward your job and your boss. Avoid the rebel at work; it will make your job a much easier one.

Absalom, being a prince and in-line to the throne, began to sway people's devotion from his father to him. After all, many of those people coming were younger than David and only knew of his exploits in the past-tense. We tend to think that anything that happened prior to our memories as being ancient history. The younger generation also often thinks themselves smarter than the older generation and so when someone of their generation comes along and says he can do a better job, it only makes sense and it is easy for the younger generation to follow one of their own.

A Family Divided

Was King David aware of what Absalom was doing? I'm sure he had to be. After all, he was king and I'm sure his advisers kept him up to speed on the tactics Absalom was employing to undermine his authority. However, why would David begin confronting one of his son's now, when he had spent his life avoiding any conflict with them? Absalom realized this and that is one of the reasons he was so bold to so openly defy his father. Also, sometimes when kids want our attention and we don't give it, they will go after it in whatever way needed, even if it hurts us.

*7 And it came to pass after forty years, that Absalom said unto the king, I pray thee, let me go and pay my vow, which I have vowed unto the LORD, in Hebron.*

*8 For thy servant vowed a vow while I abode at Geshur in Syria, saying, If the LORD shall bring me again indeed to Jerusalem, then I will serve the LORD.*

*9 And the king said unto him, Go in peace. So he arose, and went to Hebron.*

*10 But Absalom sent spies throughout all the tribes of Israel, saying, As soon as ye hear the sound of the trumpet, then ye shall say, Absalom reigneth in Hebron.*

*11 And with Absalom went two hundred men out of Jerusalem, that were called; and they went in their simplicity, and they knew not any thing.*

*12 And Absalom sent for Ahithophel the Gilonite, David's counsellor, from his city, even from Giloh, while he offered sacrifices. And the conspiracy was strong; for the people increased continually with Absalom.*

*13 And there came a messenger to David, saying, The hearts of the men of Israel are after Absalom.*

*14 And David said unto all his servants that were with him at Jerusalem, Arise, and let us flee; for we shall not else escape from Absalom: make speed to depart, lest he overtake us suddenly, and bring evil upon us, and smite the city with the edge of the sword.*

So in verse 7 Absalom goes to his father and asks to be allowed to go to Hebron so he can worship the Lord and to fulfill a vow he had made to God. Was there a vow? Was Absalom going to Hebron to worship God? At best it was partially true, at worse it was just an excuse to get out of Jerusalem so he could gather an army out of sight of his father. After all, there was no need to openly defy his father more than necessary and risk somehow provoking his father to the point David actually did his duty and put his son in his place.

So David gives his blessing to Absalom, who leaves Jerusalem heading to Hebron. He also wastes no time in sending out his messengers to Israel to let them know that Absalom was going to be their next king. The sign was when they heard the trumpet; perhaps a reference to the feasts of trumpets which began on the first day of the seventh month of the Jewish calendar. On that day, Absalom let the people know he would begin reigning as king from Hebron.

We see some of Absalom's cleverness in verse 11, where Absalom, on his way out of Jerusalem, ordered 200 soldiers to come with him. It most likely seemed to be on the spur of the moment, though in reality it was part of Absalom's planned revolt. The men left with Absalom, ignorant as to his real motives. The affect, however, was to weaken the defense of Jerusalem and render David helpless should Absalom decide to return and forcibly take the city. That is why in verse 14 David flees Jerusalem without a fight. First, he didn't want to confront his son in battle, but more importantly, even if he had his son had made sure enough soldiers were absent from the city they were supposed to defend.

Go back to verse 12 and notice who one of the conspirators was who betrayed King David and joined with Absalom. It was Ahithophel, the grandfather of Bathsheba and great-grandfather of the bastard baby that died as a result of God's intervention. He had continued to counsel David, but he was biding his time until he could get back with the man who had done evil to his family. For Ahithophel, as time passed his resentment of David grew, so that when Absalom rebelled against his father, Ahithophel was more than willing to join the rebellion.

## A Family Divided

David, who had spent so much of his early life on the run and in hiding from King Saul, is now on the run from his own son. He had come to admire his home so much, and the life of ease God had given him, that it had caused him to drift from God. Now in verse 14 he says to his household, *"Arise, and let us flee."*

How many times in the past he must have said those very words to his men as they were being pursued by Saul. He must have thought those days were over, but once again he's on the run. Why, though? Why didn't he just stay and fight. After all, he was a mighty warrior and his men valiant men. Two reasons come to mind answering that question. He had always avoided confrontation with his sons, and so the pattern had been established. But the main reason was given by David in verse 14 when he said they had to flee before Absalom brought the battle to Jerusalem and smite the city with the edge of sword. So, David left his wonderful house in the care of 10 of his concubines and left the city of David for a place far off.

*15 And the king's servants said unto the king, Behold, thy servants are ready to do whatsoever my lord the king shall appoint.*

*16 And the king went forth, and all his household after him. And the king left ten women, which were concubines, to keep the house.*

*17 And the king went forth, and all the people after him, and tarried in a place that was far off.*

*18 And all his servants passed on beside him; and all the Cherethites, and all the Pelethites, and all the Gittites, six hundred men which came after him from Gath, passed on before the king.*

Interestingly, in verse 18, six hundred men from Gath are part of those who flee with David. Gath, the city of Goliath and where David played the fool before he befriended the leader of Gath, the same leader who was going to allow David to march with him to war against Israel. That same Gath, which was so prominent in David's life, a Philistine city, had men march with David as he fled Jerusalem. David had endeared himself to the people of Gath and their loyalty was greater than that of many of his own people. Jesus Christ was rejected by his own people, yet as with the Roman Centurion, he found great faith among the Gentiles.

In times of trouble friends can be a real help. It is even a greater gift when we find out we have more friends than we think. Absalom may have rebelled against David and won the hearts of many in Israel with his charming ways, but not everyone was fooled and many stayed true to King David. When Ittai the Gittite, who had only arrived at Jerusalem the day before, left to go with David, it surprised the king who told Ittai he could return to Jerusalem , that he owed David nothing. Yet Ittai the Gittite and the men and children with him followed David.

*19 Then said the king to Ittai the Gittite, Wherefore goest thou also with us? return to thy place, and abide with the king: for thou art a stranger, and also an exile.*

*20 Whereas thou camest but yesterday, should I this day make thee go up and down with us? seeing I go whither I may, return thou, and take back thy brethren: mercy and truth be with thee.*

*21 And Ittai answered the king, and said, As the LORD liveth, and as my lord the king liveth, surely in what place my lord the king shall be, whether in death or life, even there also will thy servant be.*

*22 And David said to Ittai, Go and pass over. And Ittai the Gittite passed over, and all his men, and all the little ones that were with him.*

*23 And all the country wept with a loud voice, and all the people passed over: the king also himself passed over the brook Kidron, and all the people passed over, toward the way of the wilderness.*

*24 And lo Zadok also, and all the Levites were with him, bearing the ark of the covenant of God: and they set down the ark of God; and Abiathar went up, until all the people had done passing out of the city.*

*25 And the king said unto Zadok, Carry back the ark of God into the city: if I shall find favour in the eyes of the LORD, he will bring me again, and shew me both it, and his habitation:*

## A Family Divided

*26 But if he thus say, I have no delight in thee; behold, here am I, let him do to me as seemeth good unto him.*

*27 The king said also unto Zadok the priest, Art not thou a seer? return into the city in peace, and your two sons with you, Ahimaaz thy son, and Jonathan the son of Abiathar.*

*28 See, I will tarry in the plain of the wilderness, until there come word from you to certify me.*

*29 Zadok therefore and Abiathar carried the ark of God again to Jerusalem: and they tarried there.*

*30 And David went up by the ascent of mount Olivet, and wept as he went up, and had his head covered, and he went barefoot: and all the people that was with him covered every man his head, and they went up, weeping as they went up.*

*31 And one told David, saying, Ahithophel is among the conspirators with Absalom. And David said, O LORD, I pray thee, turn the counsel of Ahithophel into foolishness.*

*32 And it came to pass, that when David was come to the top of the mount, where he worshipped God, behold, Hushai the Archite came to meet him with his coat rent, and earth upon his head:*

*33 Unto whom David said, If thou passest on with me, then thou shalt be a burden unto me:*

*34 But if thou return to the city, and say unto Absalom, I will be thy servant, O king; as I have been thy father's servant hitherto, so will I now also be thy servant: then mayest thou for me defeat the counsel of Ahithophel.*

*35 And hast thou not there with thee Zadok and Abiathar the priests? therefore it shall be, that what thing soever thou shalt hear out of the king's house, thou shalt tell it to Zadok and Abiathar the priests.*

*36 Behold, they have there with them their two sons, Ahimaaz Zadok's son, and Jonathan Abiathar's son; and by them ye shall send unto me every thing that ye can hear.*

## Inside the House of David

*37 So Hushai David's friend came into the city, and Absalom came into Jerusalem.*

The Ark of the Covenant was taken by the priests and Levites in verse 24 to also follow David, but David told Zadok the priest to take the ark back to Jerusalem. David then took the opportunity to make Zadok and his two sons the center of his spy ring so they could inform him of Absalom's movements.

This was a sad day for not only David, but for Israel and the followers of King David as well. In verse 23 it said all the country wept. Then in verse 30 David and all the people wept as they fled.

In verse 31 someone tells him that Ahithophel, his counselor and a man in which he had placed his trust, was numbered with the conspirators. What was David's reaction to this news? He simply asked God to change the counsel of Ahithophel into foolishness. We must never forget that with God for us, who can be against us? It is interesting to see how God answered David's prayer practically at that very moment. I wonder how many times God answers our prayers almost immediately and we don't even know it. To change Ahithophel's counsel into foolishness didn't require God altering the mind of Ahithophel, it only required God placing someone else in Absalom's court who would defeat the counsel of Ahithophel.

We find that person in verse 32 when Hushai the Archite approached David in mourning for what David was suffering. David tells him that if he were to come with them he would only be a burden. He could do much more good for David if he were to go back to Jerusalem and befriend Absalom so that he could defeat Ahithophel's counsel. Hushai would be part of David's spy ring within the court of Absalom.

# Chapter 16

## Lies and Curses

*II Samuel Chapter XVI*

*1 And when David was a little past the top of the hill, behold, Ziba the servant of Mephibosheth met him, with a couple of asses saddled, and upon them two hundred loaves of bread, and an hundred bunches of raisins, and an hundred of summer fruits, and a bottle of wine.*

*2 And the king said unto Ziba, What meanest thou by these? And Ziba said, The asses be for the king's household to ride on; and the bread and summer fruit for the young men to eat; and the wine, that such as be faint in the wilderness may drink.*

*3 And the king said, And where is thy master's son? And Ziba said unto the king, Behold, he abideth at Jerusalem: for he said, To day shall the house of Israel restore me the kingdom of my father.*

*4 Then said the king to Ziba, Behold, thine are all that pertained unto Mephibosheth. And Ziba said, I humbly beseech thee that I may find grace in thy sight, my lord, O king.*

Does the Bible contain any lies? Those of the faith are usually quick to respond with a rousing, "No!" when confronted with that question. However, the answer is yes as shown in the first chapter and here is another lie in the Bible. Ziba lied to David and God recorded that lie in His Word. David, on his way of Jerusalem, meets Ziba who has a rather large gift of supplies for David and those traveling with him. When David asked Ziba where Mephibosheth was, Ziba lied when he said Mephibosheth had stayed behind because he thought Saul's line would be restored which would make him King.

Why did Ziba lie? It appears he didn't like being a servant anymore and he was going to take this opportunity to get in David's good graces and try to become the master of what belonged to Mephibosheth. Then again, maybe he was playing both sides. He left Mephibosheth behind in case Abasolom came out on top, which would give him an "in" with the new king. Notice that David does not rush to judgment against Mephibosheth. Did he know that Ziba was lying? To David it didn't matter because this wasn't the time to judge because he could take no action anyway. Now was time to flee.

*5 And when king David came to Bahurim, behold, thence came out a man of the family of the house of Saul, whose name was Shimei, the son of Gera: he came forth, and cursed still as he came.*

*6 And he cast stones at David, and at all the servants of king David: and all the people and all the mighty men were on his right hand and on his left.*

*7 And thus said Shimei when he cursed, Come out, come out, thou bloody man, and thou man of Belial:*

*8 The LORD hath returned upon thee all the blood of the house of Saul, in whose stead thou hast reigned; and the LORD hath delivered the kingdom into the hand of Absalom thy son: and, behold, thou art taken in thy mischief, because thou art a bloody man.*

*9 Then said Abishai the son of Zeruiah unto the king, Why should this dead dog curse my lord the king? let me go over, I pray thee, and take off his head.*

*10 And the king said, What have I to do with you, ye sons of Zeruiah? so let him curse, because the LORD hath said unto him, Curse David. Who shall then say, Wherefore hast thou done so?*

*11 And David said to Abishai, and to all his servants, Behold, my son, which came forth of my bowels, seeketh my life: how much*

## Lies and Curses

*more now may this Benjamite do it? let him alone, and let him curse; for the LORD hath bidden him.*

*12 It may be that the LORD will look on mine affliction, and that the LORD will requite me good for his cursing this day.*

*13 And as David and his men went by the way, Shimei went along on the hill's side over against him, and cursed as he went, and threw stones at him, and cast dust.*

So David fled Jerusalem and on his way to safety he is confronted by a descendant of Saul, Shimei. Years of resentment had built up in the man and that bitterness gushed forth on David. Abishai, one of David's mighty men and leaders, wanted to kill Shimei for his profound disrespect of the King, but David refrained Abishai and made two telling statements in doing so.

First, he said that one of his own sons was doing worse than this man, so how could he justify killing a man who was cursing him, when his own son was trying to kill him. More importantly to David, he realized Shimei was only speaking the truth and that God had bidden him to do so. Under normal circumstances the king would not have taken such insults, but these weren't normal circumstances that David now found himself under.

Nobody likes to be held accountable for their actions, especially by someone who has an intense dislike for us, but at the same time, we may not like what they have to tell us, but it still behooves us to listen to what is being said, and tune out how they are saying it.

*14 And the king, and all the people that were with him, came weary, and refreshed themselves there.*

*15 And Absalom, and all the people the men of Israel, came to Jerusalem, and Ahithophel with him.*

*16 And it came to pass, when Hushai the Archite, David's friend, was come unto Absalom, that Hushai said unto Absalom, God save the king, God save the king.*

*17 And Absalom said to Hushai, Is this thy kindness to thy friend? why wentest thou not with thy friend?*

*18 And Hushai said unto Absalom, Nay; but whom the LORD, and this people, and all the men of Israel, choose, his will I be, and with him will I abide.*

*19 And again, whom should I serve? should I not serve in the presence of his son? as I have served in thy father's presence, so will I be in thy presence.*

*20 Then said Absalom to Ahithophel, Give counsel among you what we shall do.*

*21 And Ahithophel said unto Absalom, Go in unto thy father's concubines, which he hath left to keep the house; and all Israel shall hear that thou art abhorred of thy father: then shall the hands of all that are with thee be strong.*

*22 So they spread Absalom a tent upon the top of the house; and Absalom went in unto his father's concubines in the sight of all Israel.*

*23 And the counsel of Ahithophel, which he counselled in those days, was as if a man had enquired at the oracle of God: so was all the counsel of Ahithophel both with David and with Absalom.*

In verse 14, as David and his followers continue to flee, the Bible tells us their condition was a weary one. So, they stop to refresh themselves. I'm sure the weariness was mental as well as physical. Often, the mental weariness is harder to deal with. Physically, when we are tired all our body needs is rest and it is refreshed and able to travel on in a restored fashion. But how do we refresh a weary mind?

In Matthew 11:28-29 Jesus says to come unto him and He will give us rest and refresh our souls. However, Jesus chronologically came after David, so how could David go to Jesus to have his soul refreshed? It may interest you to know that David did exactly that – he went to Jesus to have his soul refreshed when it was weary. People often go to the Psalms for encouragement, and it's those same Psalms, many of which were written by King David, that are a record of David trusting in God and going to Him for refreshment. The most famous Psalm of all, the 23$^{rd}$, says in verse 3, *"He restoreth my soul:..."*

## Lies and Curses

By focusing on God, we learn about Him. As we learn about God we find out He is trustworthy and His motive toward us is love. Once we truly understand that we can trust God in spite of our circumstances, that is when we overcome the world.

David trusted God, and now we are going to see in the rest of the chapter what God does to protect David. The actions that at the time may have seemed insignificant will eventually save David's life. Sometimes small things that happen to us, though they seem insignificant at the time, are all part of God's plan. Since we know, as it says in Romans 8:28, *"And we know that all things work together for good to them that love God, to them who are the called according to his purpose."* This verse contains two conditions that a lot of Christians gloss over. One, we must love God and two; we must be called according to his purpose. What is God's purpose? His purpose is to save the souls of men. If we love God and point to his Son Jesus Christ as the way, the truth and the life, then we fulfill those conditions and then all things will work together for good. However, just between you and God, does your life really point to Christ?

Let's look at what happens from this point in David's life to the point of his restoration in Jerusalem to see just how God works out things for good in David's life. In verse 15 we see that Ahithophel is with Absalom, David's son who was in rebellion against his father and who now had the backing of Israel. David had prayed that God would confound Ahithophel's counsel, and now we begin to see just how God is going to do that.

How many of you expected God to intervene in a direct way to confound Ahithophel's counsel? Perhaps we expected God to strike Ahithophel dumb or perform a dramatic miracle. God is working, it may not be apparent, but God is working in David's life.

In verse 16, when Hushai says to Absalom, *"God save the king, God save the king."* I'm sure Hushai was referring to David and not Absalom, even though Absalom assumed otherwise.

Hushai becomes a counselor to Absalom, and God is going to use Hushai's counsel to confound Ahithophel's. In verse 20 Absalom asks for counsel in determining what to do next. Ahithophel; therefore, counsels Absalom to openly defile ten of his father's concubines. He counsel's this to demonstrate graphically to Israel that the ties between father and son have been cut. Once Abaslom does this deed openly, no one will question if they are putting themselves in danger if they back Absalom and he later repent and return to his father. Absalom has, in the terms of Rome, crossed the Rubicon. There is no turning back.

Also, recall what it said in chapter 12 and verse 11, *"Thus saith the Lord, Behold, I will raise up evil against thee out of thine own house, and I will take thy wives before thine eyes, and give them onto thy neighbor, and he shall lie with thy wives in the sight of this sun."* Absalom, David's own son, fulfilled this prophecy.

Verse 23 is an interesting verse. It says that Ahithophel's counsel was as if he had inquired at the oracle of God. Did God tell Ahithophel to counsel Absalom to commit this gross sin against his father in order to fulfill the prophecy found in II Samuel 12:11? No, God does not counsel people to sin. God knew what Ahithophel's counsel would be, that's how he knew the prophecy would be fulfilled. Verse 23 does not say that Ahithophel's counsel came from God, it says it was *"as if"* his counsel had come from God after consulting the oracle of God.

Ahithophel had been counseling in this manner for a long time. He put on the appearance of being a man of God, but his heart was far from him. The point being, not everyone who appears to be giving the counsel of God is actually giving the true counsel of God. That is why it behooves you as a Christian to study the Word of God for yourself, so you can tell a counterfeit when you see one.

Remember, when the government trains agents to spot counterfeit bills, they don't do so by having them review the counterfeit bills, they do so by having them study the real bills so when they see a counterfeit they will realize the difference. *"Study to shew thyself approved unto God, a workman that needeth not to be ashamed, rightly dividing the word of truth."* (II Tim. 2:15)

# Chapter 17

## Confounding the Enemy

*II Samuel, Chapter XVII*

*1 Moreover Ahithophel said unto Absalom, Let me now choose out twelve thousand men, and I will arise and pursue after David this night:*

*2 And I will come upon him while he is weary and weak handed, and will make him afraid: and all the people that are with him shall flee; and I will smite the king only:*

*3 And I will bring back all the people unto thee: the man whom thou seekest is as if all returned: so all the people shall be in peace.*

*4 And the saying pleased Absalom well, and all the elders of Israel.*

*5 Then said Absalom, Call now Hushai the Archite also, and let us hear likewise what he saith.*

*6 And when Hushai was come to Absalom, Absalom spake unto him, saying, Ahithophel hath spoken after this manner: shall we do after his saying? if not; speak thou.*

*7 And Hushai said unto Absalom, The counsel that Ahithophel hath given is not good at this time.*

*8 For, said Hushai, thou knowest thy father and his men, that they be mighty men, and they be chafed in their minds, as a bear robbed of her whelps in the field: and thy father is a man of war, and will not lodge with the people.*

## Inside the House of David

*9 Behold, he is hid now in some pit, or in some other place: and it will come to pass, when some of them be overthrown at the first, that whosoever heareth it will say, There is a slaughter among the people that follow Absalom.*

*10 And he also that is valiant, whose heart is as the heart of a lion, shall utterly melt: for all Israel knoweth that thy father is a mighty man, and they which be with him are valiant men.*

*11 Therefore I counsel that all Israel be generally gathered unto thee, from Dan even to Beersheba, as the sand that is by the sea for multitude; and that thou go to battle in thine own person.*

*12 So shall we come upon him in some place where he shall be found, and we will light upon him as the dew falleth on the ground: and of him and of all the men that are with him there shall not be left so much as one.*

*13 Moreover, if he be gotten into a city, then shall all Israel bring ropes to that city, and we will draw it into the river, until there be not one small stone found there.*

*14 And Absalom and all the men of Israel said, The counsel of Hushai the Archite is better than the counsel of Ahithophel. For the LORD had appointed to defeat the good counsel of Ahithophel, to the intent that the LORD might bring evil upon Absalom.*

As stated in the last chapter, God did not confound Ahithophel's counsel through striking him dumb, or unable to reason. Verses 1-4 are a particularly good plan that would have worked if it had been carried out. We know it was good counsel on the part of Ahithophel because verse 14 says, *"The Lord had appointed to defeat the good counsel of Ahithophel."*

Just what was the good counsel? To destroy David as soon as possible while he is yet weary, and by killing the King, then all resistance to Absalom would cease. He asked for 12 thousand men to accomplish the task. We don't know how many men David had, but it is safe to say the number Ahithophel was going to attack with was greater, if not much greater, than David's number and so it would

## Confounding the Enemy

have been a good plan for the leaders of Israel, who originally had approved it.

Also, the plan was to smite the king only and to preserve the people. Smite can either mean to greatly injure or kill. In the case of David, Ahithophel most likely meant kill, because to do less would defeat the purpose of the rebellion in the first place.

Ahithophel would lead the army himself, and by doing so it would shield Absalom from having to possibly confront his father. Plus, it would keep Absalom off the battlefield and risking his life because Ahithophel knew that if to kill the King would end the resistance to Absalom, then too, to kill Absalom would end the rebellion.

By making a forced march and overtaking King David with superior numbers, the defenders of David would have to give way, meaning that David would be killed. David was hampered with taking along with him the wives and children of those remaining loyal to him; whereas, Ahithophel had no such hindrance.

It was a brilliant plan and one that would have worked, except for one small detail - God had already set in motion the plan that would confound the counsel of Ahithophel. Absalom wanted a second opinion, and so he called for Hushai.

After hearing Ahithophel's counsel and I'm sure being impressed with it, Hushai told Absalom that Ahithophel's counsel wasn't good, "at this time." The problem for Absalom is Hushai was being very honest, because the counsel wasn't good - it wasn't good for King David!

He then goes on to give other true evidence that Absalom had to agree with. David and his men were indeed mighty men. By comparing David and his men to a mother bear protecting her cubs, he was saying they would fight with ferocity. He also said David would not camp with the people and that he would be hard to find. If Absalom's men had any setbacks, then public opinion would go against him. If that were to happen, David's great reputation as a warrior would scare Absalom's army so badly that he would risk a rout.

All of this was true, except each of them had to be qualified by the circumstances. David and his men were mighty men, but now they were older and didn't have the resiliency of youth. David and his men were in flight, not posed to fight as a she-bear would be who was protecting her cubs. Finally, David didn't have time to separate himself from the people.

Hushai advises that if Ahithophel would fight and lose, that the credibility of Absalom as a leader would be crushed. In verse 10 he reminded everyone in this strategy meeting what a great warrior David was and how it might scare the army if they suffered any setbacks, and since it is a fact that David is a great warrior, those in the meeting let the emotion of fear cloud the logic of Ahithophel's counsel.

Hushai's advice to Absalom fed on Absalom's ego and also eased the fear that Hushai had cleverly introduced to the leaders of the rebellion. Gather an army large enough to leave no doubt, and for Absalom to lead the army himself, so the glory would go to him and not another, namely Ahithophel. Then, because of the overwhelming odds and the brilliant leadership of Absalom, King David could not resist such a grand army and grand leader.

Everything Hushai said made sense from an emotional standpoint; whereas, everything Ahithophel said made sense from a logical standpoint. Since Hushai, through the inspiration of God had placed the leaders of the rebellion in an emotional frame of mind, then the counsel of Ahithophel's is defeated - a defeat which will lead to Absalom's defeat.

*15 Then said Hushai unto Zadok and to Abiathar the priests, Thus and thus did Ahithophel counsel Absalom and the elders of Israel; and thus and thus have I counselled.*

*16 Now therefore send quickly, and tell David, saying, Lodge not this night in the plains of the wilderness, but speedily pass over; lest the king be swallowed up, and all the people that are with him.*

## Confounding the Enemy

*17 Now Jonathan and Ahimaaz stayed by Enrogel; for they might not be seen to come into the city: and a wench went and told them; and they went and told king David.*

*18 Nevertheless a lad saw them, and told Absalom: but they went both of them away quickly, and came to a man's house in Bahurim, which had a well in his court; whither they went down.*

*19 And the woman took and spread a covering over the well's mouth, and spread ground corn thereon; and the thing was not known.*

*20 And when Absalom's servants came to the woman to the house, they said, Where is Ahimaaz and Jonathan? And the woman said unto them, They be gone over the brook of water. And when they had sought and could not find them, they returned to Jerusalem.*

*21 And it came to pass, after they were departed, that they came up out of the well, and went and told king David, and said unto David, Arise, and pass quickly over the water: for thus hath Ahithophel counselled against you.*

*22 Then David arose, and all the people that were with him, and they passed over Jordan: by the morning light there lacked not one of them that was not gone over Jordan.*

*23 And when Ahithophel saw that his counsel was not followed, he saddled his ass, and arose, and gat him home to his house, to his city, and put his household in order, and hanged himself, and died, and was buried in the sepulchre of his father.*

*24 Then David came to Mahanaim. And Absalom passed over Jordan, he and all the men of Israel with him.*

*25 And Absalom made Amasa captain of the host instead of Joab: which Amasa was a man's son, whose name was Ithra an Israelite, that went in to Abigail the daughter of Nahash, sister to Zeruiah Joab's mother.*

*26 So Israel and Absalom pitched in the land of Gilead.*

*27 And it came to pass, when David was come to Mahanaim, that Shobi the son of Nahash of Rabbah of the children of Ammon, and*

*Machir the son of Ammiel of Lodebar, and Barzillai the Gileadite of Rogelim,*

*28 Brought beds, and basons, and earthen vessels, and wheat, and barley, and flour, and parched corn, and beans, and lentiles, and parched pulse,*

*29 And honey, and butter, and sheep, and cheese of kine, for David, and for the people that were with him, to eat: for they said, The people is hungry, and weary, and thirsty, in the wilderness.*

Now, in verse 15 we see the spy organization David had set up before he fled, put into motion and Hushai sends David a message telling him the news. However, the messengers were not without adventure. Why did God include this adventure as part of the story? Was it just for entertainment value? No, because God did not write His Word to entertain, He wrote it to impart truth.

First, Hushai gives the message to a woman to carry to the two men waiting outside the city to bring news to King David. However, a boy sees this meeting of messengers and raises the alarm by reporting what he saw to Absalom. The two messengers fled together to Bahurim. Remember Bahurim? In verse 5 of the previous chapter it was as David passed Bahurim that Shimei came out to curse David and throw stones.

In this case, however, they were hid by a woman in a well to protect those two men from the pursuers of Absalom. Why did God gives us two stories where people from the same village behaved so differently? Perhaps it is to illustrate to us that we should not judge people based on exterior factors, such as where a person lives, or a host of other factors which could include race, wealth, or education.

So, after being hid in a well by a woman, the messengers make it to King David to give their report. They advised David to flee over the Jordan River, which he did.

What was Ahithophel's reaction to Hushai's plan? He hung himself. That may seem an extreme action, but Ahithophel knew if they didn't defeat David now, they wouldn't later, so instead of being captured and punished for his rebellion, Ahithophel ended his own life.

Absalom's next mistake was to pass over Joab and appoint Amasa Captain of the Host, or leader of the army. This action would naturally upset Joab, who had a history of taking matters into his own hands. It seems that if Ahithophel had offered the post to Joab, then Joab may have joined the rebellion.

David now has time to fortify himself and rest, the very two things Ahithophel was trying to avoid with his advice. God knows what He is doing, even when we can't see it.

# Chapter 18

## Winning a Battle and Losing a Son

*I Samuel Chapter XVIII*

*1 And David numbered the people that were with him, and set captains of thousands and captains of hundreds over them.*

*2 And David sent forth a third part of the people under the hand of Joab, and a third part under the hand of Abishai the son of Zeruiah, Joab's brother, and a third part under the hand of Ittai the Gittite. And the king said unto the people, I will surely go forth with you myself also.*

*3 But the people answered, Thou shalt not go forth: for if we flee away, they will not care for us; neither if half of us die, will they care for us: but now thou art worth ten thousand of us: therefore now it is better that thou succour us out of the city.*

*4 And the king said unto them, What seemeth you best I will do. And the king stood by the gate side, and all the people came out by hundreds and by thousands.*

*5 And the king commanded Joab and Abishai and Ittai, saying, Deal gently for my sake with the young man, even with Absalom. And all the people heard when the king gave all the captains charge concerning Absalom.*

Now that Hushai had assured David time to organize his followers, David was able to go on the offensive. He organized his army into three divisions with the intention to lead them into battle against the rebels who were led by his son Absalom. However, the people thought otherwise and advised him against accompanying the army. Who were these people who advised David not to accompany the army? We get a very good idea who they were in Chapter 21 and verse 17 where they are identified as the men of David. Chapter 23 gives a list of those men who were not only the leaders of his army, but they also served as his advisers in military matters.

David often listened to his advisers and the results were usually positive. God will put people in our lives to assist us in many things, including making decisions. We need to be humble enough to listen to those people to advise us at crucial moments. They recognized that if David were captured or killed, then Absalom won. Ahithophel had also realized this simple truth, but thankfully Absalom did not heed his counsel.

Verse 5 begins with David giving an order to the leaders of the three divisions – Joab, Abishai and Ittai. Everyone heard David order these men to deal gently with Absalom. He told them to do it for his sake. In other words, he knew Absalom did not deserve mercy, but David wanted them to extend mercy to Absalom for the sake of Absalom's father, David. Surely the king would be obeyed.

*6 So the people went out into the field against Israel: and the battle was in the wood of Ephraim;*

*7 Where the people of Israel were slain before the servants of David, and there was there a great slaughter that day of twenty thousand men.*

*8 For the battle was there scattered over the face of all the country: and the wood devoured more people that day than the sword devoured.*

*9 And Absalom met the servants of David. And Absalom rode upon a mule, and the mule went under the thick boughs of a great oak, and his head caught hold of the oak, and he was taken up between the heaven and the earth; and the mule that was under him went away.*

## Winning a Battle and Losing a Son

*10 And a certain man saw it, and told Joab, and said, Behold, I saw Absalom hanged in an oak.*

*11 And Joab said unto the man that told him, And, behold, thou sawest him, and why didst thou not smite him there to the ground? and I would have given thee ten shekels of silver, and a girdle.*

*12 And the man said unto Joab, Though I should receive a thousand shekels of silver in mine hand, yet would I not put forth mine hand against the king's son: for in our hearing the king charged thee and Abishai and Ittai, saying, Beware that none touch the young man Absalom.*

*13 Otherwise I should have wrought falsehood against mine own life: for there is no matter hid from the king, and thou thyself wouldest have set thyself against me.*

*14 Then said Joab, I may not tarry thus with thee. And he took three darts in his hand, and thrust them through the heart of Absalom, while he was yet alive in the midst of the oak.*

*15 And ten young men that bare Joab's armour compassed about and smote Absalom, and slew him.*

*16 And Joab blew the trumpet, and the people returned from pursuing after Israel: for Joab held back the people.*

*17 And they took Absalom, and cast him into a great pit in the wood, and laid a very great heap of stones upon him: and all Israel fled every one to his tent.*

*18 Now Absalom in his lifetime had taken and reared up for himself a pillar, which is in the king's dale: for he said, I have no son to keep my name in remembrance: and he called the pillar after his own name: and it is called unto this day, Absalom's place.*

The great battle of this civil war that was to determine who would be king of Israel was won by David's army in the wood of Ephraim. Twenty thousand Israeli's were killed that day, which was a national tragedy. During this battle in the woods, Absalom meets his enemies and through a freak accident his head is caught in an oak tree which leaves him suspended above the ground and vulnerable.

A certain man, God does not reveal who, saw the plight of Absalom and reported it to Joab. How did Joab react? He reacted with anger at the man reporting what he saw because the man did not take advantage of the opportunity to kill Absalom. Joab knew that he was commanded by the King to preserve Absalom, but he had no intention of obeying his King. Joab knew that if Absalom was killed, the rebellion would end, so he put what he saw as the good of his men and the country as a whole above the wishes of his King.

He was even willing to reward the man if he had killed Absalom. The man reporting what had happened to Absalom put more stock in obeying his King than in receiving a reward or doing what he may have thought was right in his own eyes. By reminding Joab that everyone heard the order given by King David to deal gently with his son, Joab was without excuse for what he was about to do. The man even told Joab that King David would surly find out and when he did, it would most likely be that very same Joab that would punish the unknown man for taking the law into his own hands. Quite an irony when we consider Joab was about to do.

Joab takes three darts (http://earlyworks.weebly.com/the-cestro-sphendon---slinging-darts.html) and killed Absalom with this interesting weapon. (Follow the link provided to learn how the dart was used with a sling in ancient warfare.) The dart is a weapon that is used in a sling, so that a skilled warrior could strike his foe from a distance. It seems that Joab was so intent on killing Absalom that he took no chance he could get away and slung the darts at him from a distance. This would help to explain why in verse 15 Joab's armor bearers finished the job just in case Absalom was not dead.

Not only did Joab disobey his King by not treating Absalom gently, but Joab went so far as to slaughter Absalom in a most gruesome way. As soon as Joab knew Absalom was dead, he blew the trumpet letting his army know they could stop fighting and pursuing after the rebels, because with their leader dead the rebellion was over.

Perhaps the reason Joab had Absalom's body buried deep and covered with so many stones was an attempt to hide the body, or at least discourage anyone from digging the body up which would reveal to King David just how gruesome had been his son's death.

*19 Then said Ahimaaz the son of Zadok, Let me now run, and bear the king tidings, how that the LORD hath avenged him of his enemies.*

*20 And Joab said unto him, Thou shalt not bear tidings this day, but thou shalt bear tidings another day: but this day thou shalt bear no tidings, because the king's son is dead.*

*21 Then said Joab to Cushi, Go tell the king what thou hast seen. And Cushi bowed himself unto Joab, and ran.*

*22 Then said Ahimaaz the son of Zadok yet again to Joab, But howsoever, let me, I pray thee, also run after Cushi. And Joab said, Wherefore wilt thou run, my son, seeing that thou hast no tidings ready?*

*23 But howsoever, said he, let me run. And he said unto him, Run. Then Ahimaaz ran by the way of the plain, and overran Cushi.*

*24 And David sat between the two gates: and the watchman went up to the roof over the gate unto the wall, and lifted up his eyes, and looked, and behold a man running alone.*

*25 And the watchman cried, and told the king. And the king said, If he be alone, there is tidings in his mouth. And he came apace, and drew near.*

*26 And the watchman saw another man running: and the watchman called unto the porter, and said, Behold another man running alone. And the king said, He also bringeth tidings.*

*27 And the watchman said, Me thinketh the running of the foremost is like the running of Ahimaaz the son of Zadok. And the king said, He is a good man, and cometh with good tidings.*

*28 And Ahimaaz called, and said unto the king, All is well. And he fell down to the earth upon his face before the king, and said, Blessed be the LORD thy God, which hath delivered up the men that lifted up their hand against my lord the king.*

*29 And the king said, Is the young man Absalom safe? And Ahimaaz answered, When Joab sent the king's servant, and me thy servant, I saw a great tumult, but I knew not what it was.*

*30 And the king said unto him, Turn aside, and stand here. And he turned aside, and stood still.*

*31 And, behold, Cushi came; and Cushi said, Tidings, my lord the king: for the LORD hath avenged thee this day of all them that rose up against thee.*

*32 And the king said unto Cushi, Is the young man Absalom safe? And Cushi answered, The enemies of my lord the king, and all that rise against thee to do thee hurt, be as that young man is.*

*33 And the king was much moved, and went up to the chamber over the gate, and wept: and as he went, thus he said, O my son Absalom, my son, my son Absalom! would God I had died for thee, O Absalom, my son, my son!*

The deed has been done, and next is informing the King of the end of the rebellion and the death of Absalom. In verse 19, Ahimaaz asks Joab for permission to carry the message to King David of the day's actions and results. It is curious that Joab refused Ahimaaz permission to be the messenger, then apparently turns and gives the mission to Cushi. Why did Joab refuse permission to Ahimaaz? This is conjecture, but it seems Joab didn't trust Ahimaaz, which begs the question, why? In I Kings 1:8 Zadok the priest remained loyal to David when his other son, Adonijah planned to proclaim himself King.

Joab, Captain of the Host and one of David's mighty men, has already been seen to disobey his king. Later, he would align with Adonijah when it came time for him to try and usurp the authority of his uncle, King David. Joab appears not to have trusted Ahimaaz because he was the son of Zadok, who proved himself to be a more loyal follower of King David than Joab.

## Winning a Battle and Losing a Son

When we disobey the King, we do so in a spirit of rebellion that if not checked can lead us to hold the King in contempt. For the Christian, God is King of Kings, and when we disobey Him so deliberately it can lead to a sinful contempt against God. After all, God is merciful and rarely chastises immediately. Some, who don't know God that well, may think that God either does not know or does not care. So they continue to sin until it becomes a habitual sin. Joab's heart has slowly started to rebel against his King, and this was one of the subtle signs of his growing contempt for King David.

Ahimaaz wasn't ready to give up in his desire to carry the news to King David. Maybe he wanted David to know from his lips what had really happened, and Cushi would most likely have given a version favorable to Joab; whereas, Ahimaaz would give the truth. He asks Joab again for permission and is again denied with the empty excuse that Ahimaaz didn't have his report ready. Ahimaaz didn't let this deter him from wanting to be the messenger to King David, so he asks once more. This time, Joab felt sure that Cushi would reach David first, so he saw no harm in letting Ahimaaz go and run to tell David.

Run Ahimaaz did. He took a different route. Since it was by way of the plain, perhaps it was longer, but since the terrain would be easier to run, Ahimaaz was able to overcome the head start achieved by Cushi, through Joab, to reach King David first.

We learn in the next few verses that David and his men were very familiar with Ahimaaz, and he was trusted by them, but especially by David. There is no evidence that Cushi was recognized as Ahimaaz was, and with Ahimaaz reaching King David first, if Cushi had planned on giving David a false or misleading report, he now could not do so.

The first thing Ahimaaz does is ease everyone's mind as to the results of the battle by saying, "All is well." He then goes on to say the rebellion is over. David asks him point-blank for news of Absalom and Ahimaaz replies that he knew something had happened, but he didn't know what it was. David then tells him to step aside so he could question Cushi.

It's ironic that Joab didn't want Ahimaaz to be the messenger because he might tell David what had happened to Absalom, which could be dangerous to Joab for disobeying a direct order. Ahimaaz did not give the news of Absalom's death, that was left to Cushi who didn't know what Ahimaaz told the king, so Cushi thought it best to tell the truth. He told more of the truth than Joab expected him to do, and he did so in a tone that crushed David.

David mourned the death of his son and did so with such dramatics that everyone knew the King was hurt to the quick. Those that loved David would mourn with him, and those that felt a contempt of David, would be angered by his emotional reaction to the death of his son. Imagine how bitter a person must be to become angry at a father for mourning the death of his son.

# Chapter 19

## Contempt for the King

*II Samuel Chapter XIX*

*1 And it was told Joab, Behold, the king weepeth and mourneth for Absalom.*

*2 And the victory that day was turned into mourning unto all the people: for the people heard say that day how the king was grieved for his son.*

*3 And the people gat them by stealth that day into the city, as people being ashamed steal away when they flee in battle.*

*4 But the king covered his face, and the king cried with a loud voice, O my son Absalom, O Absalom, my son, my son!*

*5 And Joab came into the house to the king, and said, Thou hast shamed this day the faces of all thy servants, which this day have saved thy life, and the lives of thy sons and of thy daughters, and the lives of thy wives, and the lives of thy concubines;*

*6 In that thou lovest thine enemies, and hatest thy friends. For thou hast declared this day, that thou regardest neither princes nor servants: for this day I perceive, that if Absalom had lived, and all we had died this day, then it had pleased thee well.*

*7 Now therefore arise, go forth, and speak comfortably unto thy servants: for I swear by the LORD, if thou go not forth, there will not tarry one with thee this night: and that will be worse unto thee than all the evil that befell thee from thy youth until now.*

*8 Then the king arose, and sat in the gate. And they told unto all the people, saying, Behold, the king doth sit in the gate. And all the people came before the king: for Israel had fled every man to his tent.*

In the last chapter we saw evidence that Joab was drifting away from his loyalty to his king. We will now see more evidence against Joab in the first part of this chapter. For when he heard the extent that King David was mourning for his son Absalom, Joab could not control his rage toward his king.

A great victory had been won and a rebellion subdued, but King David was in mourning, and so followed the nation. After all, it was the respectful thing to do. However, since Joab had drifted away from his loyalty to his king, he was anything but respectful in verses 5 through 7. Could Joab have been feeling guilt for having been the one who killed Absalom, whom the king was now mourning so deeply? That was probably part of it. In most cases when we drift away from the one we love it comes about for various reasons, but in nearly all cases when it happens we exaggerate the negative and cover-up the positive.

Let's look at some ways Joab exaggerated the negative concerning his king. First he said that David had shamed the face of all his servants. Did David shame the face of all of them? No, I'm sure many, if not all of his servants, were genuinely mourning along with their king. When people start to use words like all and always and everyone, then that is a good sign they are trying to justify their actions by exaggerating their claims.

In verse 6 Joab goes on to claim that David loves his enemies and hates his friends. That is an obvious absurd statement, but it's also one that fueled Joab's emotional outburst.

As evidence of Joab's contempt for his king, he now orders King David to address his subjects and appease their alleged anger toward him. He doesn't just stop at ordering his king; he now threatens King David with his own rebellion.

## Contempt for the King

So, what does David do in the face of this belligerent threat? He does exactly as he's told. There may be a few reasons for this, but the one that jumps out first is that David never did like confronting those closest to him. He may also have not confronted Joab because a victory had just been won, and it was no time to have to fight another rebel. If he could appease this one, perhaps that would be better for the kingdom. We shall see later what David does to deal with Joab.

*9 And all the people were at strife throughout all the tribes of Israel, saying, The king saved us out of the hand of our enemies, and he delivered us out of the hand of the Philistines; and now he is fled out of the land for Absalom.*

*10 And Absalom, whom we anointed over us, is dead in battle. Now therefore why speak ye not a word of bringing the king back?*

*11 And king David sent to Zadok and to Abiathar the priests, saying, Speak unto the elders of Judah, saying, Why are ye the last to bring the king back to his house? seeing the speech of all Israel is come to the king, even to his house.*

*12 Ye are my brethren, ye are my bones and my flesh: wherefore then are ye the last to bring back the king?*

*13 And say ye to Amasa, Art thou not of my bone, and of my flesh? God do so to me, and more also, if thou be not captain of the host before me continually in the room of Joab.*

*14 And he bowed the heart of all the men of Judah, even as the heart of one man; so that they sent this word unto the king, Return thou, and all thy servants.*

The victory had been won and the rebellion put down, but David did not immediately return to Jerusalem, as might be expected. He didn't return even though he knew the people of Israel wanted him to be their King. Instead, he was waiting for the leaders to ask him to return as their King. Why did David want the leaders to ask him to return instead of just accepting the will of the people? He knew that if he returned against the will of the leaders, then those very same leaders would have turned the people against him. That's what leaders do – they lead.

David was not going to rule over a people who did not want him as king. The same attitude Jesus Christ took as He stood before Pilate. Jesus could have established His Kingdom by force, but He was not going to rule over a people who did not want God to rule over them. It was the leaders that rejected Jesus and as a result Jesus did not establish his kingdom, which He would have done if only the leaders of Judah had accepted Him as the king. He gave them their choice, and they rejected their Messiah.

So, in verse 11 David asked the two priests, Zadok and Abiathar, to ask the leaders of Judah why they haven't invited the king to resume his place on his throne. At this time, he also replaced Joab as the head of his army with a very unexpected choice - a choice that greatly impressed the leaders of Israel. He did not make a rash emotional decision when Joab first threatened him; he waited until not only his emotions had subsided, but also until Joab's emotions had given way. He directed the two priests to tell Amasa he has been promoted to take the place of Joab.

Do you remember who Amasa was? He was Absalom's general (Captain of the host) during the uprising. Most likely he was the one reason Joab had not joined the rebellion. Joab and Amasa were cousins, and both were nephews of King David. This also makes Absalom their cousin, so that when Absalom rebelled his cousin Amasa sided with him, instead of his uncle David.

Yet, when David had to choose the man to lead his army he chose the past traitor over his faithful friend. Why is that? Because by this time David knew Joab was no longer a faithful friend. He knew where Amasa had stood, but Joab had feigned his allegiance and willfully disobeyed King David in egregious ways. David dealt with Joab by demoting him and by placing Amasa over him. To Joab this would appear as confirmation that David loved his enemies more than his friends, but to David it shows he knew who his friend was and by this time it was not Joab.

Contempt for the King

## A Man After God's Own Heart

**Being a man after God's own heart, David was able to forgive his former enemy, and by doing so turned him into a devoted follower. The closer we are to God, the greater our power to forgive.**

So Zadok and Abiathar did as they were told, and Judah repented for their failure to invite the king back and rectified their error immediately. Therefore, David returns to Jerusalem, and on the way back some interesting things happen. At the Jordan River he is met by two well-known leaders, Shimei and Ziba. Shimei had cursed David as he fled from Jerusalem at the beginning of Absalom's revolt, and Ziba had lied about Mephibosheth so he could take over his lands. These two men had gambled David would be defeated, but now that he was returning they were very quick to come and eat crow, as the saying goes, before King David.

*15 So the king returned, and came to Jordan. And Judah came to Gilgal, to go to meet the king, to conduct the king over Jordan.*

*16 And Shimei the son of Gera, a Benjamite, which was of Bahurim, hasted and came down with the men of Judah to meet king David.*

*17 And there were a thousand men of Benjamin with him, and Ziba the servant of the house of Saul, and his fifteen sons and his twenty servants with him; and they went over Jordan before the king.*

*18 And there went over a ferry boat to carry over the king's household, and to do what he thought good. And Shimei the son of Gera fell down before the king, as he was come over Jordan;*

*19 And said unto the king, Let not my lord impute iniquity unto me, neither do thou remember that which thy servant did perversely the day that my lord the king went out of Jerusalem, that the king should take it to his heart.*

*20 For thy servant doth know that I have sinned: therefore, behold, I am come the first this day of all the house of Joseph to go down to meet my lord the king.*

*21 But Abishai the son of Zeruiah answered and said, Shall not Shimei be put to death for this, because he cursed the LORD'S anointed?*

*22 And David said, What have I to do with you, ye sons of Zeruiah, that ye should this day be adversaries unto me? shall there any man be put to death this day in Israel? for do not I know that I am this day king over Israel?*

*23 Therefore the king said unto Shimei, Thou shalt not die. And the king sware unto him.*

Shimei begs for his life in verses 19 and 20. In verse 21 Abishai, Joab's brother and nephew of David, lets it be known he thinks Shimei needs to be put to death. Notice David's reply is not just to Abishai, but it's to both Abishai and Joab. He already counted Joab an adversary, so now he was questioning whether Abishai is also going to rebel against him as Joab had already done in his heart. David lets Abishai know he is still king and as a result no one would be put to death.

Again, David shows his power to forgive. Shemei asked for David's forgiveness and David forgave. Too often, in our churches today, a member sins and the church leaders fear it may become known in the church. The member repents and asks for forgiveness, but too often the church ostracizes the member instead of forgiving him. They believe they are protecting the church from allowing sin to enter the camp, when in reality they are not practicing the forgiveness and restoration God commands.

*24 And Mephibosheth the son of Saul came down to meet the king, and had neither dressed his feet, nor trimmed his beard, nor washed his clothes, from the day the king departed until the day he came again in peace.*

*25 And it came to pass, when he was come to Jerusalem to meet the king, that the king said unto him, Wherefore wentest not thou with me, Mephibosheth?*

*26 And he answered, My lord, O king, my servant deceived me: for thy servant said, I will saddle me an ass, that I may ride thereon, and go to the king; because thy servant is lame.*

*27 And he hath slandered thy servant unto my lord the king; but my lord the king is as an angel of God: do therefore what is good in thine eyes.*

*28 For all of my father's house were but dead men before my lord the king: yet didst thou set thy servant among them that did eat at thine own table. What right therefore have I yet to cry any more unto the king?*

*29 And the king said unto him, Why speakest thou any more of thy matters? I have said, Thou and Ziba divide the land.*

*30 And Mephibosheth said unto the king, Yea, let him take all, forasmuch as my lord the king is come again in peace unto his own house.*

Ziba probably hopes he is next to speak to David, but instead Mephibosheth comes next, and his physical appearance exposes Ziba for the liar he is. Ziba had told David that Mephibosheth had sided with Absalom, but his appearance backed up his words that he had been betrayed by Ziba and that he was still a loyal servant of David, as he always had been ever since David had brought him into his household. This devotion must have been especially comforting to David, who had to deal with so much betrayal himself.

David does not punish Ziba. He seems to have already ruled that Mephibosheth and Ziba were to divide the land. After all, Ziba and his servants were doing all the work, so David thought it only fair that Ziba be able to keep a larger portion of his labor. Mephibosheth knew he didn't need the land. With David restored to his throne, all his needs would be taken care of, so he allowed all the land to go to Ziba. David had showed great kindness and forgiveness to him when he didn't think he deserved it, so he forgave Ziba and showed kindness when circumstances would suggest otherwise. That is what God asks us to do, to forgive those that trespass against us for his sake. Are we as faithful as the crippled Mephibosheth?

*31 And Barzillai the Gileadite came down from Rogelim, and went over Jordan with the king, to conduct him over Jordan.*

*32 Now Barzillai was a very aged man, even fourscore years old: and he had provided the king of sustenance while he lay at Mahanaim; for he was a very great man.*

*33 And the king said unto Barzillai, Come thou over with me, and I will feed thee with me in Jerusalem.*

*34 And Barzillai said unto the king, How long have I to live, that I should go up with the king unto Jerusalem?*

*35 I am this day fourscore years old: and can I discern between good and evil? can thy servant taste what I eat or what I drink? can I hear any more the voice of singing men and singing women? wherefore then should thy servant be yet a burden unto my lord the king?*

*36 Thy servant will go a little way over Jordan with the king: and why should the king recompense it me with such a reward?*

*37 Let thy servant, I pray thee, turn back again, that I may die in mine own city, and be buried by the grave of my father and of my mother. But behold thy servant Chimham; let him go over with my lord the king; and do to him what shall seem good unto thee.*

*38 And the king answered, Chimham shall go over with me, and I will do to him that which shall seem good unto thee: and whatsoever thou shalt require of me, that will I do for thee.*

*39 And all the people went over Jordan. And when the king was come over, the king kissed Barzillai, and blessed him; and he returned unto his own place.*

Another person was present to help conduct King David over the Jordan River, and that was Barzillai who had graciously helped David feed his people when they were in need as they fled to safety. David wanted Barzillai to go with him to Jerusalem in an attempt to somehow repay him for his timely generosity. However, Barzillai would turn the invitation down due to his old age (80) and because he said he could not be a benefit to his king, only a hindrance.

## Contempt for the King

Barzillai did concede to travel a little further with King David than he had originally planned, but when David wanted to reward him, Barzillai asked for David to bestow any reward David sought to give him, to instead give it to Chimham. Who Chimham is, or what he may have done, the Bible does not say. It is interesting to note; however, that sometimes when we are blessed it's not because of what we did to earn it, but sometimes we are blessed as a result of the grace of another.

*40 Then the king went on to Gilgal, and Chimham went on with him: and all the people of Judah conducted the king, and also half the people of Israel.*

*41 And, behold, all the men of Israel came to the king, and said unto the king, Why have our brethren the men of Judah stolen thee away, and have brought the king, and his household, and all David's men with him, over Jordan?*

*42 And all the men of Judah answered the men of Israel, Because the king is near of kin to us: wherefore then be ye angry for this matter? have we eaten at all of the king's cost? or hath he given us any gift?*

*43 And the men of Israel answered the men of Judah, and said, We have ten parts in the king, and we have also more right in David than ye: why then did ye despise us, that our advice should not be first had in bringing back our king? And the words of the men of Judah were fiercer than the words of the men of Israel.*

Verse 40 tells us that all the people of Judah, and half the people of Israel escorted the king back to Jerusalem. Now, a very curious thing happens. Not long before both Israel and Judah had risen in rebellion against David, and after the defeat of Absalom, there was a delay in requesting David to return to the throne. David had to go so far as to ask the two priests to ask Judah why they didn't ask him to be their king again. And now, while he is on his way back, the leaders of Israel and Judah start arguing over the king like two children fighting over a favorite toy. It is no wonder that it won't be long until the kingdom is divided between the northern and southern kingdoms. As Israel says in verse 43, they claimed more of David because they had ten parts in him, corresponding to the ten tribes which made up Israel. Whereas Judah had only two parts, being the tribes of Judah and Benjamin.

Israel should have been focused on the return of their king, but instead they were focused on themselves and sought their own glory. Isn't it ironic that when Jesus Christ walked on earth it was Judah in the land, and not the 10 tribes of the northern kingdom? If we focus on the king and not ourselves, then we might not become lost in our walk.

# Chapter 20

## Yet Another Revolt

*II Samuel Chapter XX*

*1 And there happened to be there a man of Belial, whose name was Sheba, the son of Bichri, a Benjamite: and he blew a trumpet, and said, We have no part in David, neither have we inheritance in the son of Jesse: every man to his tents, O Israel.*

*2 So every man of Israel went up from after David, and followed Sheba the son of Bichri: but the men of Judah clave unto their king, from Jordan even to Jerusalem.*

*3 And David came to his house at Jerusalem; and the king took the ten women his concubines, whom he had left to keep the house, and put them in ward, and fed them, but went not in unto them. So they were shut up unto the day of their death, living in widowhood.*

It seems that King David was constantly dealing with rebellion in his kingdom. After the revolt of his son, Absalom, David is confronted with yet another revolt. This time the leader is Sheba, who is described as a worthless man. He was a Benjamite, of the tribe of Saul, and like most Benjamites, it seemed he wanted no part of David. Apparently, the rest of the men of Israel felt the same way, because they all followed Sheba and forsook David.

In the previous chapter, verses 41-43 talks about Israel and Judah arguing over who had more rights to King David. Many times, we can see a type of Christ in David's life, and this is another one of those times. Jesus rode into Jerusalem on a young ass (John 12:12-

19) as the people proclaimed him King, and then, as in the case of David, he is rejected by those very same people a short time later.

Judah and Israel once again show their disagreement as Judah remains true to the King, who is of the tribe of Judah. While the whole of Israel rises in rebellion. David's grandson will be on the throne when the final political split divides Israel into the two nations of Israel (The Northern Kingdom) and Judah (The Southern Kingdom).

It is also worth noting that the territory between the Jordan River and Jerusalem remained true to King David, a territory within the borders of Benjamin. Even though the tribe of Benjamin gave David so much trouble, still his capital was located within the borders of that tribe; only five miles from his hometown of Bethlehem.

David returns to his home, the same home he had taken so much pride in, and the 10 concubines that had been defiled by Absalom were then *"put away as if they were widows."* At one time David justified to himself the taking of another man's wife to bed, but now he won't do the same to his very own concubines. David had stopped justifying wrong actions and what was right in his eyes and began doing what was right in the eyes of God.

*4 Then said the king to Amasa, Assemble me the men of Judah within three days, and be thou here present.*

*5 So Amasa went to assemble the men of Judah: but he tarried longer than the set time which he had appointed him.*

*6 And David said to Abishai, Now shall Sheba the son of Bichri do us more harm than did Absalom: take thou thy lord's servants, and pursue after him, lest he get him fenced cities, and escape us.*

*7 And there went out after him Joab's men, and the Cherethites, and the Pelethites, and all the mighty men: and they went out of Jerusalem, to pursue after Sheba the son of Bichri.*

*8 When they were at the great stone which is in Gibeon, Amasa went before them. And Joab's garment that he had put on was girded unto*

## Yet Another Revolt

him, and upon it a girdle with a sword fastened upon his loins in the sheath thereof; and as he went forth it fell out.

*9 And Joab said to Amasa, Art thou in health, my brother? And Joab took Amasa by the beard with the right hand to kiss him.*

*10 But Amasa took no heed to the sword that was in Joab's hand: so he smote him therewith in the fifth rib, and shed out his bowels to the ground, and struck him not again; and he died. So Joab and Abishai his brother pursued after Sheba the son of Bichri.*

*11 And one of Joab's men stood by him, and said, He that favoureth Joab, and he that is for David, let him go after Joab.*

*12 And Amasa wallowed in blood in the midst of the highway. And when the man saw that all the people stood still, he removed Amasa out of the highway into the field, and cast a cloth upon him, when he saw that every one that came by him stood still.*

Amasa, who had been Absalom's general, had replaced Joab as Captain of the host and now David gives him his first order, which was to assemble the men of Judah. David was mobilizing to take on the army of Sheba. Amasa goes about the job, but he tarries longer than he should have. It appears Amasa was dragging his feet, and whether this was due to a personal flaw, or a deliberate attempt to harm the cause of King David, we can't be sure. However, the result, no matter the motive, could still be catastrophic for David. Therefore, in verse six, David orders Abishai to take up the slack because if Sheba is allowed to gain the protection of a fortified city, his rebellion could be worse than Absalom's.

Abishai doesn't drag his feet as Amasa had done and leads his men out of the city in pursuit of Sheba. Included in the army is Abishai's brother, and former head of the the army, Joab. By this time Amasa joins the army and is wearing Joab's garment, which apparently would be like a uniform indicating his rank of Captain of the Host. Joab must have been a bigger man than Amasa, because the uniform fit loosely on Amasa and his sword fell out without Amasa realizing it.

It doesn't appear that Amasa was a man who could command the respect Joab commanded. He had been a rebel under Absalom, who had lost the battle in which he was the commander. Then, on his very first assignment for the king, he fails to get the job done in the time allotted. Now, as he joins the army he is careless enough to lose his sword before going into battle. Is it no wonder that Joab felt contempt for this man who had taken his place?

Joab, the mighty man of valor who had been so loyal to David was now only loyal to himself. Once again he is to deal treacherously with Amasa as he had with Abner (II Samuel 3:27). Abner had killed Joab's brother and that was the reason Joab had killed him, but he had no such personal animosity with Amasa, besides the fact he had led the rebel army that Joab's forces had defeated when Joab also killed Absalom against the express orders of King David.

David knew he had a problem with his nephew Joab, and he had tried replacing him, but Joab was going to do what was best for him and defy his king to regain what he thought was properly his, no matter what the king said. So he deceives Amasa with a kiss and kills him with his sword at a time when Amasa couldn't protect himself. He then leaves Amasa to die in the road as the army passes by. He sent an effective message to his army and anyone who may dare think they could take his place.

As Christians do we serve our king, or do we serve our self? It doesn't matter if we hold a title such as Pastor, Deacon, or Principal of a Christian school, we must be sure we are serving our king and not ourselves. With positions of authority comes power, and sometimes that power can cause those who were once good servants of the king to become more concerned with expanding their power base, or at least maintaining it, at the expense of remembering we are under the authority of God and must answer to him.

I recall working for a Christian school in Virginia where anytime the school wanted something extra from me they were quick to remind me they were a ministry, and therefore, I had to go beyond my duties to do the work they asked. However, when I needed the school to

## Yet Another Revolt

do something for me, they suddenly became a business and would not help with the needs of my family.

If you are in Christian work there should be no distinction between ministry and business. That is simply a convenient way of practicing your Christian faith when it suits you. We must be good stewards of what God has given us, but we must not lose sight of what should be our first motive which is to love God with all our heart, soul and mind, and to love our neighbor as we love our self. We must be careful not to become as Joab – serve our king when it works to our advantage and serve our self against the desire of the king, also when it works to our advantage. If we think this, then we deceive our self, because sinning against God never works to our advantage. As Galatians 6:7 says, *"Be not deceived; God is not mocked: for whatsoever a man soweth, that shall he also reap."* Remember, we're not here to serve our self, but to serve God.

*14 And he went through all the tribes of Israel unto Abel, and to Bethmaachah, and all the Berites: and they were gathered together, and went also after him.*

*15 And they came and besieged him in Abel of Bethmaachah, and they cast up a bank against the city, and it stood in the trench: and all the people that were with Joab battered the wall, to throw it down.*

*16 Then cried a wise woman out of the city, Hear, hear; say, I pray you, unto Joab, Come near hither, that I may speak with thee.*

*17 And when he was come near unto her, the woman said, Art thou Joab? And he answered, I am he. Then she said unto him, Hear the words of thine handmaid. And he answered, I do hear.*

*18 Then she spake, saying, They were wont to speak in old time, saying, They shall surely ask counsel at Abel: and so they ended the matter.*

*19 I am one of them that are peaceable and faithful in Israel: thou seekest to destroy a city and a mother in Israel: why wilt thou swallow up the inheritance of the LORD?*

*20 And Joab answered and said, Far be it, far be it from me, that I should swallow up or destroy.*

*21 The matter is not so: but a man of mount Ephraim, Sheba the son of Bichri by name, hath lifted up his hand against the king, even against David: deliver him only, and I will depart from the city. And the woman said unto Joab, Behold, his head shall be thrown to thee over the wall.*

*22 Then the woman went unto all the people in her wisdom. And they cut off the head of Sheba the son of Bichri, and cast it out to Joab. And he blew a trumpet, and they retired from the city, every man to his tent. And Joab returned to Jerusalem unto the king.*

*23 Now Joab was over all the host of Israel: and Benaiah the son of Jehoiada was over the Cherethites and over the Pelethites:*

*24 And Adoram was over the tribute: and Jehoshaphat the son of Ahilud was recorder:*

*25 And Sheva was scribe: and Zadok and Abiathar were the priests:*

*26 And Ira also the Jairite was a chief ruler about David.*

So, Joab pursues after Sheba until he finds him in Abel of Beth-maachah, where they lay siege to the city. As David's army prepares to breech the defenses of the city by erecting a ramp against their wall, a woman that the Bible describes as wise, asks to speak to Joab. Evidently she knew of Joab and his position as Captain of the Host and was not aware that King David had replaced him. That is, until Joab eliminated his rival and regained his former position without the knowledge of the king.

After making sure she was talking to the right man, she then appeals to his emotions after reminding him of the reputation of the wise counsel that came forth out of Abel. Perhaps that is why Sheba fled to this city, to seek counsel since it doesn't appear he was able to gather much of an army. The men of Israel said they were with him, but where were they now?

As part of appealing to Joab's emotions, she asks why he wants to destroy the city and the mothers within the walls. Of course, Joab responds that he doesn't want to destroy the city, but he only seeks one man – Sheba. The woman's response was that the head of Sheba would be thrown over the wall. She didn't want to take any chance that Joab would not go ahead and destroy the city, because being wise, she must have known of some of his past treachery and didn't want to risk another episode where Joab may take matters into his own hands for whatever reason.

To save the city the people of Abel take Sheba and cuts off his head and then toss it over the wall, so Joab knows that Sheba is indeed dead. This time Joab keep's his word and the army returns to Jerusalem leaving Abel intact.

The administration of David's Kingdom is listed, and we see that Joab is kept as Captain of the Hosts. Say what you will about Joab, the man got the job done. Yet David is going to keep his eyes on his commander because he knows he doesn't have his full loyalty. By acting in the flesh, it appears Joab got his way, but whereas Joab had lost faith in his king, the king had lost faith in Joab.

# Chapter 21

## Saul's Sin Visits David

*II Samuel XXI*

*1 Then there was a famine in the days of David three years, year after year; and David enquired of the LORD. And the LORD answered, It is for Saul, and for his bloody house, because he slew the Gibeonites.*

*2 And the king called the Gibeonites, and said unto them; (now the Gibeonites were not of the children of Israel, but of the remnant of the Amorites; and the children of Israel had sworn unto them: and Saul sought to slay them in his zeal to the children of Israel and Judah.)*

*3 Wherefore David said unto the Gibeonites, What shall I do for you? and wherewith shall I make the atonement, that ye may bless the inheritance of the LORD?*

*4 And the Gibeonites said unto him, We will have no silver nor gold of Saul, nor of his house; neither for us shalt thou kill any man in Israel. And he said, What ye shall say, that will I do for you.*

*5 And they answered the king, The man that consumed us, and that devised against us that we should be destroyed from remaining in any of the coasts of Israel,*

*6 Let seven men of his sons be delivered unto us, and we will hang them up unto the LORD in Gibeah of Saul, whom the LORD did choose. And the king said, I will give them.*

*7 But the king spared Mephibosheth, the son of Jonathan the son of Saul, because of the LORD'S oath that was between them, between David and Jonathan the son of Saul.*

*8 But the king took the two sons of Rizpah the daughter of Aiah, whom she bare unto Saul, Armoni and Mephibosheth; and the five sons of Michal the daughter of Saul, whom she brought up for Adriel the son of Barzillai the Meholathite:*

*9 And he delivered them into the hands of the Gibeonites, and they hanged them in the hill before the LORD: and they fell all seven together, and were put to death in the days of harvest, in the first days, in the beginning of barley harvest.*

*10 And Rizpah the daughter of Aiah took sackcloth, and spread it for her upon the rock, from the beginning of harvest until water dropped upon them out of heaven, and suffered neither the birds of the air to rest on them by day, nor the beasts of the field by night.*

*11 And it was told David what Rizpah the daughter of Aiah, the concubine of Saul, had done.*

*12 And David went and took the bones of Saul and the bones of Jonathan his son from the men of Jabeshgilead, which had stolen them from the street of Bethshan, where the Philistines had hanged them, when the Philistines had slain Saul in Gilboa:*

*13 And he brought up from thence the bones of Saul and the bones of Jonathan his son; and they gathered the bones of them that were hanged.*

*14 And the bones of Saul and Jonathan his son buried they in the country of Benjamin in Zelah, in the sepulchre of Kish his father: and they performed all that the king commanded. And after that God was intreated for the land.*

It would appear that now all will be well in David's kingdom, but instead we find the country in a three-year drought. What had David done to deserve this? The answer is nothing. Israel was going

## Saul's Sin Visits David

through a drought because of the actions of Saul. However, Saul was dead and so why punish Israel now?

Sometimes bad things happen to us that are not our fault. Conversely, sometimes good things happen to us that we do not deserve. We are quick to complain to God when the former happens but remain silent when the latter occurs.

When bad things happen to us is it okay to question God? David did. But wait! Isn't questioning God evidence of a lack of faith? No. When we question why God does something, it shows our faith in Him because we are seeking to understand what it is God is trying to teach us. Notice: however, that David is not blaming God, he is simply questioning why the drought is happening, and God answers him. There is a huge difference between questioning God and blaming God.

When God answers David's question as to why Israel was suffering through a drought, we discover it is because of the actions of the now deceased King of Israel - Saul. Why? The answer is because he slew the Gibeonites in his zeal for Israel and Judah. What was wrong with that, after all, isn't it good to have a zeal for God? At first reading that may appear to have been all Saul was doing; however, his zeal wasn't for God, he slew the Gibeonites to make himself look better to his people. He was seeking his own glory and not the glory of God. A treaty had been made and Saul broke that treaty, therefore, the entire nation was punished.

The treaty in question is found in Joshua Chapter 9. The Gibeonites had deceived Israel into making a treaty with them where Israel promised not to harm them. Vows are so important to God that He shows us through the deception of the Gibeonites that we are to honor our word even if we were deceived in doing so. When Saul broke that vow through slaying an unknown number of Gibeonites, then God brought judgment upon Israel. Yet that judgment wasn't immediate. It makes us wonder why God waited to punish Israel until David was king. Had David done anything wrong? Let's move on and perhaps we will find out.

David wanted to know what he had to do to set the matter straight, so he went to the offended party and asked. The price was seven of

Saul's sons to be hanged for the death and destruction their father had brought upon them. They didn't want monetary reparations or land or the lives of innocent Israelites, and apparently they didn't consider Saul's sons to be innocent. That, or those who Saul slew were considered innocent by the Gibeonites, so it then became a matter of hurting those who hurt them, no matter the apparent lack of complicity.

David chose seven sons of Saul, whom it turned out to be two sons through a concubine and five grandsons, since all the sons of Saul had been killed expect for Mephibosheth, whom David would not deliver to the Gibeonites because of his vow with Jonathan, Mephibosheth's father and the son of Saul.

Five of the grandsons were raised by Michal, the daughter of Saul who had been David's first wife. She raised the five sons of Adriel and Merab, the daughter of Saul whom Saul had promised to David as a wife if he fought the Philistines for him. Saul had reneged on the promise and given Merab to Adriel instead, and now their five sons would be given to the Gibeonites to satisfy the wrong that had been done to them. Think on that for a minute. David was giving over the five sons of the woman who was supposed to have been his first wife - the same five sons that were raised by Merab's sister Michal, who was indeed David's first wife; meaning that David was the step-father to the adopted sons of the woman who was supposed to be his first wife.

Sometimes when we read about the deaths of people in the Bible we may forget the lives touched by these deaths. Yet seven sons of Saul were hanged, and they belonged to two mothers. One of those mothers, Rizpah, mourned for her two sons, and that mourning touched the heart of David. In response he gathered the bones of Saul and Jonathan, and the rest of those of Saul's house who had been killed and gave them a proper burial. You may recall that in chapter two David commended the men of Jabesh-gilead for their action of rescuing the bodies of Saul and Jonathan from off the wall where they had been put on display by the Philistines. He asked God to bless them and told them if they ever needed anything to let him know. I

## Saul's Sin Visits David

stated in chapter two that we often tell those in need we'll pray for them and let us know if they need anything, but we fail to put action behind our words. Sometimes it takes a mourning mother to remind the greatest of us, such as David, where our duty lies and show compassion when we sometimes forget our own humanity.

Back to one of our above questions that still needs answered. Had David done something wrong to make God bring the drought upon Israel in response to the actions of Saul? God was not punishing David as a person; he was punishing Israel as a nation because of the actions of the king of Israel. David was the succeeding king, and so he was responsible to make things right as the king for the actions of the past king. If we as a nation elect leaders that do ungodly things, then we the people of that nation can suffer the consequences of the actions of those ungodly leaders.

The Gibeonites were satisfied because David had done as he promised, and more importantly God was satisfied. As a result of setting things straight, not only with the Gibeonites, but with the proper burial for those of the house of Saul, God lifted the drought and rain returned to the land.

*15 Moreover the Philistines had yet war again with Israel; and David went down, and his servants with him, and fought against the Philistines: and David waxed faint.*

*16 And Ishbibenob, which was of the sons of the giant, the weight of whose spear weighed three hundred shekels of brass in weight, he being girded with a new sword, thought to have slain David.*

*17 But Abishai the son of Zeruiah succoured him, and smote the Philistine, and killed him. Then the men of David sware unto him, saying, Thou shalt go no more out with us to battle, that thou quench not the light of Israel.*

*18 And it came to pass after this, that there was again a battle with the Philistines at Gob: then Sibbechai the Hushathite slew Saph, which was of the sons of the giant.*

*19 And there was again a battle in Gob with the Philistines, where Elhanan the son of Jaareoregim, a Bethlehemite, slew the brother of Goliath the Gittite, the staff of whose spear was like a weaver's beam.*

*20 And there was yet a battle in Gath, where was a man of great stature, that had on every hand six fingers, and on every foot six toes, four and twenty in number; and he also was born to the giant.*

*21 And when he defied Israel, Jonathan the son of Shimea the brother of David slew him.*

*22 These four were born to the giant in Gath, and fell by the hand of David, and by the hand of his servants.*

Does this mean that peace now comes to David's kingdom? Not as long as the Philistines were around. If you recall, David had fled to Gath when Saul was pursuing him, which seemed ironic because that was the hometown of Goliath. Apparently the sons of Goliath were too young to seek their revenge on David, but now they've grown and become warriors in their own right. They also possessed the size of their father, and one of them sought to slay David in battle. The ravages of age catch up with us all, and David was no exception. The mighty warrior that had slain so many now almost becomes the victim himself and it was apparent to all those around that David had lost a step, as the saying goes.

Abishai, the brother of Joab, saves David's life and then the men of David make him swear to stay home from battle, because if something were to happen to the king it would throw the entire kingdom into turmoil.

Yet there are still giants to slay. David, as a young man, had done what no one else in the army of Israel had been willing to do - he had fought Goliath. Not only had he fought him, but he defeated him. David's leadership and courage had inspired Israel and now through the rest of chapter 21 the remaining brothers and sons of Goliath, who are still challenging Israel, fall in battle one by one. When the time came for Israel to face their own giants, they did so and prevailed.

# Chapter 22

## Song of Deliverance

*II Samuel XXII*

*1 And David spake unto the LORD the words of this song in the day that the LORD had delivered him out of the hand of all his enemies, and out of the hand of Saul:*

*2 And he said, The LORD is my rock, and my fortress, and my deliverer;*

*3 The God of my rock; in him will I trust: he is my shield, and the horn of my salvation, my high tower, and my refuge, my saviour; thou savest me from violence.*

*4 I will call on the LORD, who is worthy to be praised: so shall I be saved from mine enemies.*

*5 When the waves of death compassed me, the floods of ungodly men made me afraid;*

*6 The sorrows of hell compassed me about; the snares of death prevented me;*

*7 In my distress I called upon the LORD, and cried to my God: and he did hear my voice out of his temple, and my cry did enter into his ears.*

*8 Then the earth shook and trembled; the foundations of heaven moved and shook, because he was wroth.*

*9 There went up a smoke out of his nostrils, and fire out of his mouth devoured: coals were kindled by it.*

*10 He bowed the heavens also, and came down; and darkness was under his feet.*

*11 And he rode upon a cherub, and did fly: and he was seen upon the wings of the wind.*

*12 And he made darkness pavilions round about him, dark waters, and thick clouds of the skies.*

*13 Through the brightness before him were coals of fire kindled.*

*14 The LORD thundered from heaven, and the most High uttered his voice.*

*15 And he sent out arrows, and scattered them; lightning, and discomfited them.*

This chapter would appear to be better suited for Psalms than for II Samuel, but of course, a large part of this does comes directly from Psalms. David's life seems to be one of turmoil and constant struggle, and we sometimes wonder how he made it through so much tribulation. The fact that he wrote so many of the Psalms, and that some of them appear here in II Samuel should give us a good clue. David didn't focus on himself, he focused on God. He didn't sit around and whine about his own problems, but he constantly reminded himself who God is. When you start to struggle in your faith, remind yourself who God is and what God has done.

Who was the foundation of David's life? Where did he go to for strength and refuge? Who was it that delivered David from his troubles? David knew the answer was God, and he showed God his thanks by being inspired to write many of the Psalms that reveal God to us today.

As God reveals his attributes through the Psalms, he also reveals Christ to us, and this Psalm, which is the same as Psalm 18, I feel is one of those chapters that reveals a moment in the life of Christ that is very important.

## Song of Deliverance

Have you ever wondered what was going on in the spirit world as Jesus Christ hung suffering on the cross? What was Satan doing and what was God doing? I once had a professor in college who stated if he ever repeated himself it was because what he was saying must be important. Since this chapter can also be found in the Psalms, then I think it's safe to say that God wants us to pay attention. This is more than a song of deliverance for a difficult time in David's life; it's THE song of deliverance for when God sacrificed himself for the sins of the world.

When Christ was praying in the Garden of Gethsemane, he could very well have been praying this Psalm. In the mystery of the triune God, Jesus Christ was falling into the safety and security of God's arms. Verse 5 and 6 reveals how Jesus was feeling as he had the sins of the entire world placed on him.

Verse 7

In his distress he called upon God, and God heard him out of his temple. Imagine God in his temple as his son cries to him from his creation in the throes of pain and with the weight of the sins of the world upon him.

Verse 8

As Christ died on the cross, there was a great earthquake (Matthew 27:51). Verse 8 tells us that the earth shook and trembled; the foundations of heaven moved and shook because he was wroth. Not only was there a great upheaval in the earth and in heaven, but the spiritual world shook at the death of the Son of God.

Verse 9

God's anger was so fierce that smoke went up out of his nostrils and a devouring coal of fire went out and devoured. I can imagine the demons buzzing around the cross taunting the Son of God in their euphoria for having defeated God. This would have been a part of the suffering of Jesus – the taunting of Satan and the fallen angels. God allowed this to happen, but the time came when enough was enough. God's anger devours them, and the demons are scattered. God would only allow his son to suffer for so long.

Verse 10

God came down from heaven and the heavens bent as darkness was between Him and earth. Matthew 27:45 tells us that darkness was over all the land for the space of three hours. Unbeknownst to those there at the time, God was there over his son scattering the demons with his arrows of fire and lightening's. Read verses 9 through 15 and imagine this happening as Mary and the others looked on.

Satan had thought he won a great victory, but at this display of wrath from God, imagine the look on Satan's face as he realized his error. It's a terrible thing to fall into the hands of an angry God!

The taunting demons were driven away, and God delivered Christ from his enemies. When Christ rose from the dead he not only conquered death, but Satan's defeat and fate were sealed. Acts 13:33 tells us that it was at the resurrection of Jesus Christ that he was begotten. When God says that Jesus Christ is his only begotten son, he's not referring to his birth, but rather his resurrection. Jesus Christ was begotten when he rose from the dead, which completed His work of salvation.

While Jesus walked this earth, he was not known as Jesus Christ, but rather, Jesus of Nazareth. He was called Master and Rabbi, but not the Messiah, or Christ, which is the Greek form of Messiah. It is only after he is begotten or raised from the dead that the Word of God refers to the Son of God as Jesus Christ.

*16 And the channels of the sea appeared, the foundations of the world were discovered, at the rebuking of the LORD, at the blast of the breath of his nostrils.*

*17 He sent from above, he took me; he drew me out of many waters;*

*18 He delivered me from my strong enemy, and from them that hated me: for they were too strong for me.*

*19 They prevented me in the day of my calamity: but the LORD was my stay.*

*20 He brought me forth also into a large place: he delivered me, because he delighted in me.*

*21 The LORD rewarded me according to my righteousness: according to the cleanness of my hands hath he recompensed me.*

*22 For I have kept the ways of the LORD, and have not wickedly departed from my God.*

*23 For all his judgments were before me: and as for his statutes, I did not depart from them.*

*24 I was also upright before him, and have kept myself from mine iniquity.*

*25 Therefore the LORD hath recompensed me according to my righteousness; according to my cleanness in his eye sight.*

*26 With the merciful thou wilt shew thyself merciful, and with the upright man thou wilt shew thyself upright.*

*27 With the pure thou wilt shew thyself pure; and with the froward thou wilt shew thyself unsavoury.*

*28 And the afflicted people thou wilt save: but thine eyes are upon the haughty, that thou mayest bring them down.*

Verses 16 through 25 talks of how God delivered Christ in his hour of need. Just as he delivers us in our hour of need. Does that mean that God spared the life of His Son? Not at all, but He did comfort Him and walk with Him during that time. It is true that God turned his back on Jesus as part of the penalty for sin, but once the price was paid and the atonement accomplished, then God delivered the messiah. We get a sense of the fellowship between father and son in these verses and it's sweet. It's also comforting to know that we can have that same kind of fellowship with God.

Verses 26-28 shows us a little more about the heart of God. He shows himself merciful to those that show mercy, and upright to those that are upright. Are we judgmental of those that struggle with sin, or do we show them mercy? If we want God to be merciful to us and our shortcomings, then it behooves us to be merciful toward others and their shortcomings.

Too often our churches are guilty of unrighteous indignation. We discover a church member is not perfect and we are quick to judge and to shun. "Did you hear about brother so and so? I always knew there was something wrong with him." Then, in a show of superiority the local church army marches out the wounded brother and shoots him. We must keep the church pure we argue in our pride, not realizing the church is made up of sinners. Where is the mercy?

Notice in these verses the one attribute that sticks out because it's different. God is merciful to the merciful; upright to the upright, pure to the pure, but the difference is he's not froward to the froward. To the froward God is unsavory. The difficult and contrary find God's sweet savor to be a bitter pill to swallow, because it exposes their own bitterness.

*29 For thou art my lamp, O LORD: and the LORD will lighten my darkness.*

*30 For by thee I have run through a troop: by my God have I leaped over a wall.*

*31 As for God, his way is perfect; the word of the LORD is tried: he is a buckler to all them that trust in him.*

*32 For who is God, save the LORD? and who is a rock, save our God?*

*33 God is my strength and power: and he maketh my way perfect.*

*34 He maketh my feet like hinds' feet: and setteth me upon my high places.*

*35 He teacheth my hands to war; so that a bow of steel is broken by mine arms.*

*36 Thou hast also given me the shield of thy salvation: and thy gentleness hath made me great.*

*37 Thou hast enlarged my steps under me; so that my feet did not slip.*

## Song of Deliverance

*38 I have pursued mine enemies, and destroyed them; and turned not again until I had consumed them.*

*39 And I have consumed them, and wounded them, that they could not arise: yea, they are fallen under my feet.*

*40 For thou hast girded me with strength to battle: them that rose up against me hast thou subdued under me.*

*41 Thou hast also given me the necks of mine enemies, that I might destroy them that hate me.*

*42 They looked, but there was none to save; even unto the LORD, but he answered them not.*

*43 Then did I beat them as small as the dust of the earth, I did stamp them as the mire of the street, and did spread them abroad.*

*44 Thou also hast delivered me from the strivings of my people, thou hast kept me to be head of the heathen: a people which I knew not shall serve me.*

*45 Strangers shall submit themselves unto me: as soon as they hear, they shall be obedient unto me.*

*46 Strangers shall fade away, and they shall be afraid out of their close places.*

*47 The LORD liveth; and blessed be my rock; and exalted be the God of the rock of my salvation.*

*48 It is God that avengeth me, and that bringeth down the people under me,*

*49 And that bringeth me forth from mine enemies: thou also hast lifted me up on high above them that rose up against me: thou hast delivered me from the violent man.*

*50 Therefore I will give thanks unto thee, O LORD, among the heathen, and I will sing praises unto thy name.*

*51 He is the tower of salvation for his king: and sheweth mercy to his anointed, unto David, and to his seed for evermore.*

Now let's pick up in verse 29 and the picture is of God being a light onto our path. He gives us strength when surrounded by enemies and enables us to escape. David is praising and worshiping God, and this is a very good thing for us to do also. When we pray, if you don't already, begin your prayer by telling God how great He is. When you realize how great God is, and how trustworthy He is, and how much He loves you, then our problems seem to melt away as we realize God is able and willing to overcome for us.

As Christians we should be confident, but not self-confident. Our confidence needs to come through God, not because of how great we are, but because of how great He is. David was not a perfect man, as I am sure you have seen by now. What set David apart was his faith and his heart, which was in tune with God's heart. I suggest you go back and find those italicized paragraphs titled, "A Man After God's Own Heart," and see if your heart matches God's heart. If not, take time to pray to God and ask him to give you His heart. God says in James 1:5 *"If any of you lack wisdom, let him ask of God, that giveth to all men liberally, and upbraideth not; and it shall be given him."* The heart of God is wisdom and to have His heart is to have peace.

When God delivers us and gives us the strength to overcome our enemies that is when we need to praise Him and worship Him. In the remainder of this chapter you can see how David worships God. Let us do the same.

# Chapter 23

## Rosebud

*II Samuel XXIII*

*1 Now these be the last words of David. David the son of Jesse said, and the man who was raised up on high, the anointed of the God of Jacob, and the sweet psalmist of Israel, said,*

*2 The Spirit of the LORD spake by me, and his word was in my tongue.*

*3 The God of Israel said, the Rock of Israel spake to me, He that ruleth over men must be just, ruling in the fear of God.*

*4 And he shall be as the light of the morning, when the sun riseth, even a morning without clouds; as the tender grass springing out of the earth by clear shining after rain.*

*5 Although my house be not so with God; yet he hath made with me an everlasting covenant, ordered in all things, and sure: for this is all my salvation, and all my desire, although he make it not to grow.*

*6 But the sons of Belial shall be all of them as thorns thrust away, because they cannot be taken with hands:*

*7 But the man that shall touch them must be fenced with iron and the staff of a spear; and they shall be utterly burned with fire in the same place.*

The Orson Welles movie, "Citizen Kane," is widely known as the greatest movie ever made. The movie revolves around Charles Foster Kane's last words, which was simply "Rosebud." The whole movie is based upon searching for the meaning of that one word. After all, as the movie states, the dying words of a man must be especially important. Imagine how important are the dying words of a king who is known for being a man after God's own heart.

A person would think that the last words of David would be found in the last chapter, but this is only the next to last chapter, which makes me wonder what is coming next. The chapter begins with what we might expect as an epitaph on his tombstone. He is recognized as the son of Jesse and a man whom God raised up on high. He is also noted as the anointed of God, and not just any god, but the God of Jacob. He is called the sweet Psalmist and his work is identified as being given to him by God through the inspiration of the Spirit.

Allow me, if you will, to write the above as if it were on a tombstone.

Here lies David, the son of Jesse. King of Israel through the grace of God. Songwriter and author of the Book of Psalms through the inspiration of the Holy Spirit.

What we know as David's last words is what we would call his secret to success. There are many books known as self-help books that are written to show us how to have success. David's secret to success is actually God's secret to success, so it behooves us to know what the creator of the universe has to say about what so many find elusive. Below is a summary of David's last words as he gives us the secret to success.

Success for the person in a leadership position first means we have to be just. This is more than a sense of fair-play, it's ruling over others from a Godly perspective knowing that as a leader we will answer to God on how we treated those under us.

Just as the morning is a new day and time of refreshing, so must a leader be. We set the tone for the day and our manner should be pleasant and refreshing to the point it causes those under us to grow as people.

A leader realizes what he is not a result of his own hard work, but it is the result of the grace of God. A leader without the salvation of God through Christ cannot lead properly because he cannot properly fear God. Sure, he can have successes, but those successes will never be complete or lasting. A Godly leader will not be perfect, but to be a proper leader he must put God first.

A leader cannot waste his time worrying about what troublemakers and naysayers might say; therefore, a leader relies on God to confound the foolish. However, we must still protect ourselves from mean spirited people and be ready to defend our faith when the time comes. How do we know when that time has come? If God is truly first in our lives, then he will give us the strength for the fight, and the proper timing.

Verse 7 tells us to be fenced with iron and to carry the staff of a spear. Refer to Ephesians 6:10-20 to see the New Testament version of this sage advice. Being fenced with iron is the defensive protection of the breastplate of righteousness and the shield of faith. Also, we are to wield the double-edged sword, which is the Word of God.

*8 These be the names of the mighty men whom David had: The Tachmonite that sat in the seat, chief among the captains; the same was Adino the Eznite: he lift up his spear against eight hundred, whom he slew at one time.*

*9 And after him was Eleazar the son of Dodo the Ahohite, one of the three mighty men with David, when they defied the Philistines that were there gathered together to battle, and the men of Israel were gone away:*

*10 He arose, and smote the Philistines until his hand was weary, and his hand clave unto the sword: and the LORD wrought a great victory that day; and the people returned after him only to spoil.*

*11 And after him was Shammah the son of Agee the Hararite. And the Philistines were gathered together into a troop, where was a piece of ground full of lentiles: and the people fled from the Philistines.*

*12 But he stood in the midst of the ground, and defended it, and slew the Philistines: and the LORD wrought a great victory.*

*13 And three of the thirty chief went down, and came to David in the harvest time unto the cave of Adullam: and the troop of the Philistines pitched in the valley of Rephaim.*

*14 And David was then in an hold, and the garrison of the Philistines was then in Bethlehem.*

*15 And David longed, and said, Oh that one would give me drink of the water of the well of Bethlehem, which is by the gate!*

*16 And the three mighty men brake through the host of the Philistines, and drew water out of the well of Bethlehem, that was by the gate, and took it, and brought it to David: nevertheless he would not drink thereof, but poured it out unto the LORD.*

*17 And he said, Be it far from me, O LORD, that I should do this: is not this the blood of the men that went in jeopardy of their lives? therefore he would not drink it. These things did these three mighty men.*

*18 And Abishai, the brother of Joab, the son of Zeruiah, was chief among three. And he lifted up his spear against three hundred, and slew them, and had the name among three.*

*19 Was he not most honourable of three? therefore he was their captain: howbeit he attained not unto the first three.*

*20 And Benaiah the son of Jehoiada, the son of a valiant man, of Kabzeel, who had done many acts, he slew two lionlike men of Moab: he went down also and slew a lion in the midst of a pit in time of snow:*

*21 And he slew an Egyptian, a goodly man: and the Egyptian had a spear in his hand; but he went down to him with a staff, and plucked the spear out of the Egyptian's hand, and slew him with his own spear.*

*22 These things did Benaiah the son of Jehoiada, and had the name among three mighty men.*

*23 He was more honourable than the thirty, but he attained not to the first three. And David set him over his guard.*

Verse 8 begins the mention of David's mighty men. One of the lessons here as that no man does it alone. When God raised David up, one of the ways He did so was through the means of mighty men of valor. An old saying goes, "It's not what you know, it's who you know." That is very true, but we must first know God, after all, imagine who God knows. If we pick our "mighty men," then we may pick the wrong ones. However, if we allow God to provide us those we need to be successful, then He knows them much better than we do. They will not be perfect, but if we treat them right, then we have strong men who, in our modern language, "Have our back."

Verses 13 through 19 give us an interesting story that shows us just how dedicated David's men were to him. David, as if thinking out loud wished for water from the well of Bethlehem. Not just any well, but the one by the gate. He did not order his men to obtain the water, nor did he even suggest it. However, three of his mighty men loved David, who wasn't even the recognized king yet, so much that they risked their lives to simply please him.

What was David's response to this mighty act of love? He poured the water on the ground! At first glance this might seem extremely rude and selfish; however, the opposite was true. The water really was precious to David, precious enough even that three men risked their lives to obtain it. David knew these men risked their lives to obtain that water, and it greatly disturbed him. The water wasn't worth the life of even one of his men; therefore, he poured it on the ground as an offering to God. The act of the three men was appreciated because it showed their love and loyalty, but at the same time it was foolish, and David didn't want his men doing foolish things to please him. To put it a bit more simply, things aren't important, people are.

*24 Asahel the brother of Joab was one of the thirty; Elhanan the son of Dodo of Bethlehem,*

*25 Shammah the Harodite, Elika the Harodite,*

*26 Helez the Paltite, Ira the son of Ikkesh the Tekoite,*

*27 Abiezer the Anethothite, Mebunnai the Hushathite,*

*28 Zalmon the Ahohite, Maharai the Netophathite,*

*29 Heleb the son of Baanah, a Netophathite, Ittai the son of Ribai out of Gibeah of the children of Benjamin,*

*30 Benaiah the Pirathonite, Hiddai of the brooks of Gaash,*

*31 Abialbon the Arbathite, Azmaveth the Barhumite,*

*32 Eliahba the Shaalbonite, of the sons of Jashen, Jonathan,*

*33 Shammah the Hararite, Ahiam the son of Sharar the Hararite,*

*34 Eliphelet the son of Ahasbai, the son of the Maachathite, Eliam the son of Ahithophel the Gilonite,*

*35 Hezrai the Carmelite, Paarai the Arbite,*

*36 Igal the son of Nathan of Zobah, Bani the Gadite,*

*37 Zelek the Ammonite, Naharai the Beerothite, armourbearer to Joab the son of Zeruiah,*

*38 Ira an Ithrite, Gareb an Ithrite,*

*39 Uriah the Hittite: thirty and seven in all.*

The remainder of the chapter goes on to list the mighty men and even tell a few of their deeds. It also shows the organizational set-up which was part of David's administration. One thing you may notice as you read this list is that not all of David's mighty men were Israelites. One of those notable exceptions is found in verse 39 where the last of his mighty men were mentioned, and it is none other than Uriah the Hittite. The very same Uriah that David dealt so unjustly with; so much so that he had him killed so he could obtain his wife – Bathsheba.

When David had wished aloud for the water of Bethlehem, once it was brought to him by his mighty men, he was sensitive enough to the potential sacrifice his men had made to make the water a sacrifice to God and refuse to drink it. However, after David drifted away from God he became selfish to the point that he sacrificed one of his mighty men to gain that which did not belong to him. If it could happen to David, it could happen to any of us, and that is one of the reasons we need to remain humble before God and seek his will and not our own.

# Chapter 24

## Subtraction by Addition

*II Samuel XXIV*

*1 And again the anger of the LORD was kindled against Israel, and he moved David against them to say, Go, number Israel and Judah.*

*2 For the king said to Joab the captain of the host, which was with him, Go now through all the tribes of Israel, from Dan even to Beersheba, and number ye the people, that I may know the number of the people.*

*3 And Joab said unto the king, Now the LORD thy God add unto the people, how many soever they be, an hundredfold, and that the eyes of my lord the king may see it: but why doth my lord the king delight in this thing?*

*4 Notwithstanding the king's word prevailed against Joab, and against the captains of the host. And Joab and the captains of the host went out from the presence of the king, to number the people of Israel.*

*5 And they passed over Jordan, and pitched in Aroer, on the right side of the city that lieth in the midst of the river of Gad, and toward Jazer:*

*6 Then they came to Gilead, and to the land of Tahtimhodshi; and they came to Danjaan, and about to Zidon,*

*7 And came to the strong hold of Tyre, and to all the cities of the Hivites, and of the Canaanites: and they went out to the south of Judah, even to Beersheba.*

*8 So when they had gone through all the land, they came to Jerusalem at the end of nine months and twenty days.*

*9 And Joab gave up the sum of the number of the people unto the king: and there were in Israel eight hundred thousand valiant men that drew the sword; and the men of Judah were five hundred thousand men.*

At first glance it would appear that God moved David to sin because it says in verse 1 that God moved David to say, "Go, number Israel and Judah." In verse 10 David confesses his sin to God and called it a great sin. Did God cause David to sin?

Man has free will and God does not interfere with the will of man. There is no sin in God; therefore, not only can God not sin, he cannot cause man to sin. The sin was already in David's heart and by God moving David it simply means the circumstances were ripe in David's life to choose to sin. Circumstances created by David.

God will sometimes change our circumstances to help us not to sin, and sometimes God allows circumstances to take place that will reveal our true faith in God, as he did with Job.

What was the circumstance that revealed David's faith in God at the time? Obviously, it must have been a time of peace, which seemed to be rare in David's kingdom. The root of the sin, as is the root in so many of our sins, was pride. David was the king of an expanding empire. It would be easy to think it was his cunning and keen mind which led to the victories, but as we saw in the previous chapter, it was God that raised David up, not David.

David's reasoning probably ran something like this - It would be good to know how many men are available for combat in case I need to raise an army. It would also be good if I had a job for my men to do instead of having them be idle. If I know how many men I can put in the field, then if I am confronted with an enemy, I know what my resources are.

The above is all sound logic in the world's eyes, but we are not of this world, and neither is our God. David was to trust God, not in

## Subtraction by Addition

the size of the human army he could command. His strength lay in his faith in God, not his army.

Ironically, it was Joab in verse 3 that questioned the king on the wisdom of numbering the people, declaring that God could and would provide however many men were needed for any occasion. Joab's fault was doing what was best for Joab and killing anyone who stood in his way. However, in spite of those faults it did not mean he didn't possess a faith in God. Sometimes Christians find it easier to have faith in God for the big things apart from us personally, but when it comes to having faith in God for our own personal issues, we fall short, as Joab did.

So Joab and the other mighty men travel around the country conducting a census as told to do by their king. It took 9 months and 20 days and by the end of it David was to discover Israel had 800,000 they could put in the field and Judah possessed 500,000 men.

Could there have been an ulterior motive for David to number Israel and Judah separately? After all, Israel was not a reliable supporter of their king, as is witnessed by their failures to accept him as their king and instead follow one of Saul's son, Ishibotheth. Maybe David was looking forward to the possibility of Civil War, which actually did happen after his death.

*10 And David's heart smote him after that he had numbered the people. And David said unto the LORD, I have sinned greatly in that I have done: and now, I beseech thee, O LORD, take away the iniquity of thy servant; for I have done very foolishly.*

*11 For when David was up in the morning, the word of the LORD came unto the prophet Gad, David's seer, saying,*

*12 Go and say unto David, Thus saith the LORD, I offer thee three things; choose thee one of them, that I may do it unto thee.*

*13 So Gad came to David, and told him, and said unto him, Shall seven years of famine come unto thee in thy land? or wilt thou flee three months before thine enemies, while they pursue thee? or that there be three days' pestilence in thy land? now advise, and see what answer I shall return to him that sent me.*

*14 And David said unto Gad, I am in a great strait: let us fall now into the hand of the LORD; for his mercies are great: and let me not fall into the hand of man.*

*15 So the LORD sent a pestilence upon Israel from the morning even to the time appointed: and there died of the people from Dan even to Beersheba seventy thousand men.*

Once the census was over, the Bible says David's heart smote him. God will convict us of our sin if we are open to allowing God to speak to us. When he does we can either put our head in the sand as a form of denial, or we can repent of our sin and ask God's forgiveness.

In the case of Uriah, God used the prophet Nathan to expose David's sin to him since he had his head in the sand and wasn't open to the direct conviction of God. In this instance David's sin was exposed by God, but he sent Gad to him to make it clear to David what he needed to do make things right again with God.

I had a Pastor in Florida who used to say, "We can choose our sins, but we can't choose our consequences." That is nearly always true, but in this case God granted David a choice of one of three possible consequences to his sin. The one David chose shows his understanding of the nature of God.

The three consequences God gave David to choose from was a seven-year famine, a three-month time on the run, or 3 days of pestilence. The country had just gone through a 3-year famine if this was indeed about the same time as the famine mentioned in Chapter 21. David had already spent a great deal of his time on the run from somebody, whether it be Saul, the Philistines, or his own son. The final choice was 3 days of pestilence. Time wise the final choice would be best, so that coupled with David's hope for God's mercy and wanting to take man out of the equation, made it his final choice.

To begin with, 7 years of famine would lead to further consequences that there would be no way of knowing just how severe things could get. Plus, people can go to extreme measures in extreme times, so

## Subtraction by Addition

David couldn't be sure what they might do when they were forced to suffer for so long. 3 months of fleeing an enemy would be something David had experience with, and after those 3 months David would win the victory, but again, a lot can happen in 3 months. Men can be very cruel and the longer they have to be cruel the more cruel they can be. However, 3 days of pestilence, though it could be bad, David knew that God's mercy could also be great, and that people would not have had time to lash out at whatever or whomever they wanted to blame. For 7 years of famine it might take 4 years for his mercy to relieve the situation, or with 3 months of fleeing it might take God 2 months before his mercy overcame his anger. Therefore, even if God chose not to be merciful, 3 days of pestilence would keep the reaction of people out of the equation, so to David 3 days of pestilence became preferable.

Jonathan Edwards preached the famous sermon, "Sinners in the Hands of an Angry God," which led to the first Great Awakening in what would become the United States. David reasoned it was better to fall into the hands of an angry God than an angry mob. God would be just and merciful, mobs rarely are.

Therefore, God sent his angel to destroy 70,000 men throughout Israel. Yes, God is a God of love, but He is also a God of justice. Without justice there can be no love.

It's interesting to consider that those that died were of Israel, and not Judah. So, unless Israel included Judah in these numbers, it was Israel that was weakened by this plauge.

When the angel came to the city God loved – Jerusalem. God showed his mercy as David had hoped. David didn't know when, where, or even if God would show his mercy, but he hoped. If God had not stayed the angel from continuing the judgment, He would have still been right in what He did.

I don't know how many more were to have died if God hadn't showed mercy, but I could guess either 10,000 more, or 60,000. I would first think 10,000 and I come up with that number because another 10,000 added to 70,000 would equal 10% of the 800,000 David numbered in Israel. There is no way of knowing if that is true, and it doesn't take into account those numbered in Judah, but one thing I am sure of is that the 70,000 who died did so for a reason and purpose and it wasn't just a random number.

*16 And when the angel stretched out his hand upon Jerusalem to destroy it, the LORD repented him of the evil, and said to the angel that destroyed the people, It is enough: stay now thine hand. And the angel of the LORD was by the threshingplace of Araunah the Jebusite.*

*17 And David spake unto the LORD when he saw the angel that smote the people, and said, Lo, I have sinned, and I have done wickedly: but these sheep, what have they done? let thine hand, I pray thee, be against me, and against my father's house.*

*18 And Gad came that day to David, and said unto him, Go up, rear an altar unto the LORD in the threshingfloor of Araunah the Jebusite.*

*19 And David, according to the saying of Gad, went up as the LORD commanded.*

*20 And Araunah looked, and saw the king and his servants coming on toward him: and Araunah went out, and bowed himself before the king on his face upon the ground.*

*21 And Araunah said, Wherefore is my lord the king come to his servant? And David said, To buy the threshingfloor of thee, to build an altar unto the LORD, that the plague may be stayed from the people.*

*22 And Araunah said unto David, Let my lord the king take and offer up what seemeth good unto him: behold, here be oxen for burnt sacrifice, and threshing instruments and other instruments of the oxen for wood.*

*23 All these things did Araunah, as a king, give unto the king. And Araunah said unto the king, The LORD thy God accept thee.*

*24 And the king said unto Araunah, Nay; but I will surely buy it of thee at a price: neither will I offer burnt offerings unto the LORD*

## Subtraction by Addition

*my God of that which doth cost me nothing. So David bought the threshingfloor and the oxen for fifty shekels of silver.*

*25 And David built there an altar unto the LORD, and offered burnt offerings and peace offerings. So the LORD was intreated for the land, and the plague was stayed from Israel.*

God has a purpose in everything He does. Even the place where God told the angel to stop became very significant, and it's significant to this very day (Including whatever day it is that you are reading this). God allowed David to see the angel, and when He did the angel was at a specific place on the property of a man named Araunah. David didn't know that God had already told the angel to stop, and so David pleaded with God to punish him and not the people for his transgression. Sometimes God answers our prayers even before we ask them.

Back to the significance of where the angel stopped, and the judgment of God was over. David bought that spot, at the threshing floor of Araunah, and built an alter on the spot after buying the land. This place became the Temple Mount and it's where Solomon's Temple, and later Herod's Temple, stood. It's now the area near where the Dome of the Rock, the Muslim Temple, now stands in Jerusalem. It is also the place where Jesus Christ is going to set one foot on when he comes back and reveals himself to Israel at the end of the Great Tribulation. Again, God has a purpose for everything He does.

One last note about David buying this land from Araunah, and then this being the spot where he built an altar, and later the temple. Many Muslim leaders deny that this land was ever the site of the Temple, let alone that it ever belonged to Israel. The book of II Samuel was written roughly a thousand years before the Muslim religion was even born and the Quran written. The land was bought in a recorded legal transaction and God recorded it over three thousand years before the Muslim's, who are now denying the land belonged to Israel, and have vowed to drive Israel into the sea.

Probably for a long-time people wondered why God went into so much detail about this legal transaction, and now after thousands of years it is becoming clearer. Once again, God has a purpose for everything He does.

It is not for us to know the purpose. It is for us to trust and obey. David's life shows us what happens when we put God first, and what happens when we fail to do so. Let us all resolve to seek God from this day forward.

# Appendix

## Trial of the Amalekite

Setting: Ziklag, the city given to David by the Philistines as his own while he was in exile from Israel as a result of the actions of King Saul.

Characters: David, The Amalekite, and The Egyptian

The sketch begins after the Amalekite enters Ziklag and is brought before David for questioning.

**Scene One**

David: Where did you come from?

Amalekite: (vs 3) Out of the camp of Israel.

David: How did the battle go?

Amalekite: (vs 4) Israel fled and was defeated, and King Saul and Jonathan are dead.

David: How do you know that King Saul and Jonathan are dead?

Amalekite: (vs 6-10) I just happened to be at Mt. Gilboa, and I saw King Saul was worn out and trying to escape. He was being chased by men on horses and chariots and they were gaining ground. When he looked behind him, he saw me and called to me. I asked him what he wanted, and he asked me who I was. I told him I was an Amalekite, and he told me to kill him because he didn't want to be captured alive. I knew he couldn't escape, so I did what he asked and killed him. I brought you his crown and his bracelet.

David: Who are you?

Amalekite: (vs 13) An Amalekite.

David: Whose side did you fight on in the battle?

Amalekite: (vs 3) Israel.

David: So, you're saying you're an Amalekite that fought on the side of Israel?

Amalekite: Yes.

David: You may step down. I call the Egyptian to the stand. (After the Egyptian takes his seat on the stand.) Who are you?

Egyptian: (I Samuel 30:13) An Egyptian, the servant of an Amalekite who left me for dead.

David: Where did the Amalekites, who left you, go?

Egyptian: (I Samuel 30:14) They invaded Judah.

David: Let me remind the Jury that Judah is a part of Israel, so in truth the Amalekites were invading Israel. (Returns to questioning the Egyptian.) What did they do to Ziklag, the city given to me and where we are now?

Egyptian: (I Samuel 30:14) They burned it.

David: Once again, let me remind the jury the Amalekites invaded Israel ,whose King was Saul and Jonathan was his son, and that this man now on trial claiming to have fought on the side of Israel is also an Amalekite. (Turning to the Amalekite) You may return to the stand. (After the Amalekite sits down.) Where did you say you were when you saw King Saul?

Amalekite: (vs 6) On Mt. Gilboa.

David: And what did you say Saul was doing when you saw him?

Amalekite: (vs 6) He was fleeing.

David: So, he was being pursued?

Amalekite: (vs 6) Yes.

## Trial of the Amalekite

David: What did Saul do when he was being pursued?

Amalekite: (vs 7) He looked behind him and saw me and called to me.

David: You say he looked behind him?

Amalekite: Yes.

David: (Focusing closely on the Amalekite) If Saul looked behind him when he called for you, wouldn't that put you among his pursuers?

Amalekite: (Hesitates to answer.)

David: Let's go on. What did King Saul ask you to do?

Amalekite: (vs 9) To kill him.

David: Did you kill him?

Amalekite: (vs 10) Yes.

David: Were you not afraid to kill the Lord's anointed? (Puts up his hand indicating the Amalekite does not have to answer the question, and then asks another.) How did you come into possession of the crown and bracelet?

Amalekite: (vs 10) I took them.

David: Why did you take them?

Amalekite: (vs 10) So I could bring them to you.

David: No more questions. You may step down. (Turning to the jury.) Ladies and Gentlemen of the Jury, by this man's own admission he is an Amalekite. We have heard testimony that the Amalekites invaded Israel and fought on the side of the Philistines. This very city, Ziklag, which belongs to us, was burned by those very same Amalekites. This Amalekite claimed to be fighting on the side of Israel, but he is an enemy and not a friend. By his own admission he claimed to be behind Saul, the same position as Saul's pursuers. By his own admission he claims to have killed the King of Israel and stolen the crown and King's bracelet. He claimed to be bringing the crown and bracelet to me but let me remind you that Ziklag is between Israel and the land of the Amalekites. To travel from the battlefield back home, he had to pass through here. Since the Amalekites had already burned the place, he thought it was safe to assume it would be deserted and the best and safest route back home. Was his intention to bring me King Saul's bracelet? The answer is no. To him, the crown and bracelet were just spoils of war. So, who is this man? He's an enemy of Israel who fought for the Philistines and who claims to have killed our King and stolen his crown. Therefore, I put it to the jury to render its sentence.

Jury: (In unison read verse 16.)

Verse 16 is David's judgment, as was his to lawfully make, against the Amalekite for his crimes against the nation of Israel. He had proven the man's guilt beyond a reasonable doubt, and just as God is a just God, and David is a King after God's own heart, and thus just, he brought judgment against the man for his crimes. That judgment included the penalty, which was death.

Some say that the love of God would prevent him from sending anyone to hell. However, there can be no love without justice. God, in his great love, provided a way to escape that ultimate justice through his Son, who took the blame for our sin and paid the ultimate price – death. He then, in His great love, gave us freedom of choice as to whether we accept that pardon or if we refuse the mercy He offers us. To accept His pardon, simply pray to God and ask Him to forgive you of your sins and tell him you are accepting the pardon He offers through His Son, Jesus Christ, who paid for your sins when he died on the cross and rose again.

If you are sincere and believe that God can save you out of Hell and into Heaven, through the sacrifice of the death and resurrection of His Son, then you are born again and have just become a new creature in Christ.

www.ingramcontent.com/pod-product-compliance
Lightning Source LLC
Chambersburg PA
CBHW072154100526
44589CB00015B/2228